Praise for
LOVE & SEX

"So many couples struggle in their sexual lives because they divide sex and love, which never works. True sexual fulfillment only really works in the context of intimacy and love; intimacy and love express themselves in the completeness of sexual fulfillment. Nancy Houston has written an excellent, practical, and very hopeful book on how to reintegrate the division. *Love & Sex* is highly recommended."

—John Townsend, Ph.D., *New York Times* bestselling author of *Boundaries*, founder of the Townsend Institute for Leadership and Counseling, and psychologist

"Without question, one of the greatest communicators of our generation on Christian sex and intimacy is Nancy Houston."

—Amy Ford, president of Embrace Grace and author of *A Bump in Life*

"*Love & Sex: A Christian Guide to Healthy Intimacy* is a must read! Nancy Houston communicates with excellence the meaning of healthy intimacy in a relevant and natural way. You will be drawn into the compelling stories as you discover truth upon truth regarding this hot topic. As fully restored pastors who have overcome the impact addiction to pornography and betrayal has had upon our marriage, we know from our own experience that many people will find hope while reading this incredible book. We believe without a doubt that Nancy's encouraging and insightful words will help many take that next step in opening up and reaching out with their own struggles and into the ultimate freedom God has in store for them."

—James and Teri Craft, authors, recovery coaches, and co-founders of The Novus Project

"In *Love & Sex: A Christian Guide to Healthy Intimacy,* Nancy Houston uses storytelling in a powerful way to bring insight, healing, and revelation to the deepest and most complex issues of sexuality."

—Jimmy Evans, founder and CEO of Marriage Today

"Nancy Houston unlocks all the tough questions on sex for both men and women. There are no barriers she won't break through. We have literally watched the lights go on in the hearts of both men and women as she unfolds the reasons behind unhealthy behaviors and fears regarding our sexuality.

"In a world filled with perversion of truth surrounding this subject, Nancy shines a brilliant light through the darkness. Read this book, then give it to everyone you know! For future generations' freedom from taboos, for marriages—*Love & Sex*."

> —Paul Cole, president of the Global Fatherhood Initiative, and Judi Cole, a talented artist and founder of the One Heart Brunch

"*Love & Sex* is a book that addresses one of the most important and confused aspects of our humanity. In this book Nancy Houston gives solid, practical, professional, biblical advice and perspective on a subject that affects everyone. A must read for those engaged and a resource for the rest of us working to live out our marriage commitment in loving connection with each other."

> —Tom Lane, lead executive senior pastor/Dallas campus pastor at Gateway Church

"My friend Nancy Houston has helped me redeem my sexuality in such a godly way. After being molested as a child I coped with that pain by viewing pornography. For years I viewed sex and sexuality through a lens God never intended. Nancy has helped me understand God's plan and perspective about sex and my sexuality and I have been freed to enjoy it with my wife in ways I could never have imagined! *Love & Sex: A Christian Guide to Healthy Intimacy* will help you understand love and sex God's way. The right way. The fun way. ENJOY!"

> —Tim Ross, senior pastor at Embassy City Church

LOVE & SEX

LOVE
AND
SEX

A CHRISTIAN GUIDE TO
HEALTHY INTIMACY

Nancy Houston
LICENSED PROFESSIONAL COUNSELOR AND
CERTIFIED SEX THERAPIST

REGNERY
FAITH

Regnery™ is a trademark of Salem Communications Holding Corporation; Regnery® is a registered trademark of Salem Communications Holding Corporation

Unless otherwise noted, Scripture quotations are taken from THE MESSAGE, copyright © 1993, 1994, 1995, 1996, 2000, 2001, 2002 by Eugene H. Peterson. Used by permission of NavPress. All rights reserved. Represented by Tyndale House Publishers, Inc.

Scripture quotations marked NLT are taken from the Holy Bible, New Living Translation, copyright ©1996, 2004, 2007, 2013, 2015 by Tyndale House Foundation. Used by permission of Tyndale House Publishers, Inc., Carol Stream, Illinois 60188. All rights reserved.

Cataloging-in-Publication data on file with the Library of Congress

ISBN 978-1-62157-675-4
e-book ISBN 978-1-62157-715-7

Published in the United States by
Regnery Faith, an imprint of
Regnery Publishing
A Division of Salem Media Group
300 New Jersey Ave NW
Washington, DC 20001
www.RegneryFaith.com

Manufactured in the United States of America

10 9 8 7 6 5 4 3 2 1

Books are available in quantity for promotional or premium use. For information on discounts and terms, please visit our website: www.Regnery.com.

The Author is represented by Ambassador Literary Agency, Nashville, TN.

CONTENTS

To my husband, Ron.
Without you, this book wouldn't be possible.
Thank you for loving me, encouraging me, and pushing me to be
braver than I would be without you. I love doing life with you;
even when we fight we find our way back to each other's arms.
Your love holds me steady and allows me to explore this
beautiful life we share!

Introduction

God had us in His heart when He created the world. He wanted a playground for His children to discover and explore the mysteries and intricacies of the heavens above and the earth below. Mostly, He wanted His creative design to draw us deeper into intimate knowing with Him. To top off His artful display, He created males and females with longings, desires, needs, and the potential to share bodies in sexual intimacy. Our human sexual drives aren't a mistake or a glitch in our engineering, even though I'm pretty sure all of us have wondered at times, "Why is this so complex?" STDs, rape, assaults, sexual confusion, abuse...well the list could go on and on about how we humans have misused this beautiful, nearly majestic part of our bodies, souls, and spirits in ways that haven't enhanced our lives.

Rather than taking a clinical peek into human sexuality, or attempting to describe God's glorious plan for these sexual

bodies of ours, I have chosen to tell a story. A story of very real
people (no character is based on a person, but rather a character
sketch of intermingled lives) and how they were shaped sexually,
because we are all shaped sexually, even if we have never taken
an honest look at how that shaping went. As we follow their
stories, we will meet the people they have loved, desired, and
married, and how they have hurt and betrayed each other. We
will also discover how sexuality either enhanced that love connection or destroyed it.

My prayer is this book will capture your attention, engage
your mind, and mostly expand your heart to discover the
goodness of God's design in creating you—a sexual creature.
May you find healing in the pages your fingers are wrapped
around.

What might you find within these pages?

- How our histories shape our sexuality
- A deeper understanding of sexual trauma
- How to build a sexually satisfying marriage
- Abuse, porn, sexual confusion, affairs, and other
  hard stuff
- Integrating spirituality with sexuality
- Permission to have fun, creative, erotic, married
  sex
- The role of love and sex
- Accepting and making room for differences in
  sexuality
- The role of friendship and attachment in healthy
  sexuality

THROUGH MY EYES

For nearly twenty years of my life, I have worked with beautiful humans who have struggled with their sexuality. I have shed tears with those who have experienced the dark side of what God meant for good. I've helped those who lost hope and mostly created a safe place for women and men to find hope and healing. I've helped them to discover they too can experience a happy, playful, even erotic, married-sex life. This topic is more than just clinical for me; I too have walked through significant pain to find the joy in understanding and even claiming my sexuality as a valuable jewel of who I am as a person. I hope you will do the same.

ONE

The Invitation

Have you ever wondered why your sexuality is important or if it has a purpose? God designed us as sexual creatures with a purpose in mind. He meant it for good: as a way to know Him more fully. Our sexuality is a window into our Creator; He loves passionately, He designed us to be His beloved bride, and He wanted a way for humans to reproduce and to express their love for the one they have committed their lives to in a unique and special way. God wanted married love to have a sexual expression, which separates it from all other love. He designed our bodies with hormones and a sexual nervous system with sexual body parts. He decided to give men a body part to fit within the female body and a female organ that has the capacity to not only give birth to another human being but to receive a man with pleasure. Attraction, sexual urges, and desire are all part of our wiring. When you really think about how our bodies fit together and are drawn toward one another, it is some sort of miracle. Only God could have come up with this master plan. We learn of God's wondrous story in Genesis 2:

> God formed man out of dirt from the ground and blew into his nostrils the breath of life. The man came alive— a living soul! Then God planted a garden in Eden, in the east He put the Man he had just made in it. God made all kinds of trees grow from the ground, trees beautiful to look at and good to eat. The Tree-of-Life was in the middle of the garden, also the Tree-of-Knowledge-of-Good-and-Evil (Gen. 2:7–9).
>
> God took the Man and set him down in the Garden of Eden to work the ground and keep it in order. God commanded the Man, "You can eat from any tree in the garden, except from the Tree-of-Knowledge-of-Good-and-Evil. Don't eat from it. The moment you eat from that tree, you're dead" (Gen. 2:15–17).

God said, "It's not good for the Man to be alone; I'll make him a helper, a companion" (Gen. 2:18). In other texts it says God will make him a helpmeet, God uses this term several times to describe a woman and many more times to describe Himself. God calls Himself our HelpMeet. This shows the female is not less than male, but equal to and different from the male.

> So God formed from the dirt of the ground all the animals of the field and all the birds of the air. He brought them to Man to see what he would name them. (God empowered Man to influence, name, create and act.)

> Whatever the Man called each living creature, that was
> its name. The Man named the cattle, named the birds
> of the air, named the wild animals; but he didn't find a
> suitable companion (Gen. 2:19–20).

What a task God gave to Adam! I believe part of what God was doing here was to help Man develop an awareness of his aloneness. I imagine as Man named the animals, he must have noticed there were two of the same kind—one with male parts and the other with female parts. I also imagine he watched them frolic and mate and wondered where his playmate and partner was. We humans often don't notice a need until we become *aware*. God didn't assign a random task to Adam, but created a life changing event for the dawning of awareness of Man's desire for a complementary counterpart.

God loves to meet our needs, so He proceeds to put Man into a semi-coma. "God put the Man into a deep sleep. As he slept he removed one of his ribs and replaced it with flesh. God then used the rib that he had taken from the Man to make Woman and presented her to the Man" (Gen 2:21–22).

I can only imagine Man's thrill at God's presentation. As a matter of fact, he exclaims, "Finally! Bone of my bone, flesh of my flesh! Name her Woman for she was made from Man" (Gen. 2:23–24). Can you hear his joy? At last, finally, he has someone like himself!

He then prophesies, "Therefore a man leaves his father and mother and embraces his wife. They become one flesh" (Gen. 2:24). He recalls the animals and how they are partnered with one like themselves, but slightly different from each other. He must have envied how they had one another, a companion, a sexual partner who brought not only pleasure, but offspring. Now God has made him one of these. He is delighted and can instantly imagine how this partner will cause him to change his priorities to make room for her in his life. I think he also recognizes her as his sexual partner and must be experiencing sexual arousal for the first time. Then Scripture tells us, "The two of them, the Man and his Wife, were naked, but they felt no shame" (Gen. 2:25).

Here is where the sad part of the story enters. God made everything so good for the Man. He set him in paradise, everything was perfect except for one thing and that one thing was the man didn't have a counterpart. So God, being the good Father He is, already had a plan in place to take care of and provide everything the man would need. We know the plan was in place before He even made Man in that He actually extracts the female from the male. They were there together, sharing one body, but they had no way to enjoy the other, unless the one became two. God is a *one-times-two* kind of God who loves to take two and make them one, and yet the one still remains two. He is a relational God and we humans are made in His image and purposed to be relational creatures, just like our Designer.

The two had the freedom to play, explore, and discover the over three hundred erogenous zones God gave each of them. They could frolic and enjoy one another's bodies with absolutely not one drop of shame. Scripture says, "No shame," even, "Naked and not ashamed." It's all so good, man and woman living together in paradise, the way God intended it to be. And then the serpent, the evil one, enters the story and the beautiful plan God created took a nasty turn.

"The serpent was clever, more clever than any wild animal God had made. He spoke to the Woman: "Do I understand that God told you not to eat from any tree in the garden?" (Gen. 3:1). He has the nerve to start with a lie, just a little white lie to create doubt, to wedge in just a sliver of unbelief, questioning God's goodness. God hadn't said any tree, only one tree. I imagine there were thousands to pick from, only one did God set a boundary around.

The Woman said to the serpent, "Not at all. We can eat from the trees in the garden. It's only about the tree in the middle of the garden that God said, 'Don't eat from it; don't even touch it or you'll die'" (Gen. 3:2–3). Do you see how the serpent exaggerated? He loves to make God sound like the bad guy, the cheapskate, the withholder of fun stuff.

The serpent told the Woman, "You won't die. God knows that the moment you eat from that tree, you'll see what's really going on. You'll be just like God, knowing everything ranging all the way from good to evil." (Gen. 3:4–5) He forgot to mention God is good and wanted to provide *good* for His children and protect them from the burden of evil.

Sadly, the Man is silent during the exchange, and neither the Man nor the Woman bother to consult with God. Consider if they would have looked at each other and said, "Hey, God has a stellar track record with us. He has only provided wondrous things for us, we live in paradise, we eat organic fruits and veggies, we swim whenever we want to, and we have a lot of fun together. We have never experienced Him withholding anything good from us. Let's wait—He should be here soon—and we can talk this over with Him before we listen to this creepy snake." But Man remained silent and Woman acted on her own.

We see the same scenario today, with male and female and what harms our relationships with each other. The serpent planted doubt in Woman, and every woman has been marked by doubt since then. We ask ourselves, "Is God really good? Can I trust Him? Maybe I should take things into my own hands— maybe if I have sex with this guy he will love me and give me the love I so hunger for? Maybe he will be faithful to me, if I give him everything I have?" Or, "I don't need a man or relationships. I can make it on my own."

Because this is a book on sexuality, I will point out how the Fall affected our sexual decision making. First, the Man was passive. Passivity paralyzes a man and leaves him feeling inade- quate, feeling less than; in extremes, he begins to believe he is a loser. Some men get stuck in either one of two shame-inducing extremes. Either too fearful to even approach a female or, if he happens to find a woman, he hides himself from her, believing if she knew the real him she would run. Or he spends his life trying to prove his masculinity through sexual conquests—proving to himself and others that he is indeed adequate.

The story continues, "When the Woman saw that the tree looked like good eating and realized what she would get out of it—she'd know everything!—she took and ate the fruit and then gave some to her husband, and he ate" (Gen 3:6). Yep, now we know it all. Lucky us, instead of male and female having paradise and a lot of sexual fun together in a committed, covenantal, safe relationship, now we have a lot of heartache; because when she ate, we all ate, and our eyes have been opened to evil, and sometimes it looks pretty tempting, especially before we count the cost of the consequences of shame.

Let's face it, sex is fun, and orgasms are amazing! But having sex with someone who doesn't care about you eventually leaves you either hurt and lonely, or hard and closed off or both. Before I sound like I am judging Eve, let me say if I were in her shoes, I most likely would have made the same choice. I hate to think that given what we know now, but let's be honest; we all have a tendency to do what seems like a good idea at the moment without counting the cost. And we are easily sold.

Immediately the two of them did, "See what's really going on,"—saw themselves naked. They sewed fig leaves together, as makeshift clothes for themselves. Naked was normal and naked with no shame was their *shared* normal. Yet they eat of evil and the first awareness is one that radically shifts their sexuality. I often wonder if our sexuality is at the deepest core of who we are as human beings, and if that is why the enemy of our God goes after it with dirty vengeance. You might wonder, why was their nakedness the first thought? Why not, "My heart hurts, or I feel somehow different, or the sky is a different shade of blue, or where is Father—help, Daddy!!"

No, what hits them is, "You are naked and I am naked and that's not good, so let's cover our sexual parts and let's hide." There is a radical shift in their once joyful, vulnerable, creative relationship. Now the focus has changed to hiding from their shared shame. They cut parts of themselves off from each other and the process of isolation, hiding, and independence becomes their new normal. They move from a position of "we" into an

"I" stance with themselves and with God. "When they heard the sound of God strolling in the garden in the evening breeze, the Man and his Wife hid in the trees of the garden, hid from God" (Gen. 3:8).

We have been hiding ourselves from each other and from God ever since. God made us for relationships; the biggest lie of the enemy of our soul is we are grossly inadequate and we must figure out life on our own. He says we are shameful for not *knowing*.

It's no wonder we are lonely and one-night stands, casual hookups, and sexual withholding in married life have become the norm. People who hide are lonely. It doesn't fit our DNA, because we were made for knowing and being known. What was meant to be natural to us humans—relationships and genuine knowing and healthy sexual relating—becomes unnatural. Lest I sound like a total pessimist, let's not forget Jesus came to set it all right for us. What we made a mess of, He came to totally redeem and to put back in place the Father's original plan.

"God called to the Man: 'Where are you?'" The God of pursuit has come looking for His beloved children. Adam replies, "'I heard you in the garden and I was afraid because I was naked. And I hid.' God said, 'Who told you, you were naked?'" (Gen. 3:9–11).

This is such a powerful question, a question that begs exploring. I wonder if God is saddened when a parent slaps his or her child's hand because they are exploring their genitals and learning that they feel good. I wonder if God is saddened when a teenager's body is flooded with either testosterone or estrogen and sexual feelings arise and someone says, "What is wrong with you? Your sexuality is dirty, and you better keep that under wraps. Don't come home pregnant, young lady; and buddy, you better keep that in your pants."

Imagine if naked were normal and we weren't freaked out that God made us sexual creatures on purpose? Imagine if we saw our sexuality as normal, but sacred, and the act of sex as something godlike and holy and fun and playful? We'd live in a different world where we would talk about sex and educate our children and integrate our values and our spirituality into the greater context of our *sexuality*.

It would be normal to include God in our sexual decision making. Our choices would be less about what our hormones are saying and more about our character structure. But because of the Fall we have separated our sexuality from our spirituality, and we keep much of what we do with it hidden under the fig leaves—away from God and away from those we are meant to love.

If our sexuality and spirituality were integrated, we might have frequent conversations with God such as; "God, would You teach me how to make love to my husband? I just haven't been in the mood lately, and the kids are wearing me out. I don't want to have someone grab my breasts, snuggle me, or tug on me. I need some space, and sex just doesn't sound like fun."—Or— "God, I need Your help in connecting sexually with my wife. I seem to be all thumbs, and I'm not touching her in a way that stirs much up. Would You help me, help us to have the kind of sex You want us to have?"

If single, we might say, "Lord, I am dating this amazing person, and I am so hot on fire for him or her sexually. What do

I do with my desires and longings? How do I handle wanting to have sex so bad—and yet You want me to wait until we are in a covenant relationship. How do I do this?"

The point is we wouldn't be alone. God is not ashamed of our sexual struggles; He wants to help us. Adam and Eve didn't have to be alone when they were tempted. And we don't have to settle for passivity, or doing it on our own. God is here and wants to be a part of your sexual life so you don't end up in the blame/shame cycle like Adam and Eve got caught up in or tempted beyond what you can handle.

"The Man said, 'The Woman you gave me as a companion, she gave me fruit from the tree, and, yes, I ate it.'" (Gen. 3:12) He has to take responsibility for at least the part where he opened his own mouth and took a bite. I mean, he has experienced God as intelligent, so surely he can't hand her all of the blame. Yes, for sure, the majority of the blame, he reasons, belongs to the Woman. What he must have praised his God for earlier in chapter two of Genesis, he is now blaming God for, "After all God", he reasons, "You are the one who stuck me with her. I didn't ask for her." The amazing gift God gave Man suddenly became a liability and his emotions for his darling companion turned to contempt.

"God said to the Woman, 'What is this that you've done?'" (Gen. 3:13) A common parenting moment is happening here. "Why'd you hit your brother? You cheated on your wife? You lied to your husband? What?" God is attempting to engage with the woman's neurobiology. She has gone into her primal brain and His question is intended to help her find her prefrontal cortex, the smart, reasoning, adult part of her brain.

She is oh-so-human and replies, "The serpent seduced me...and I ate." (Gen. 3:13) How easily we are seduced by things that aren't good for us. Tempted by the sexy coworker, tempted to turn away from our spouse instead of moving toward relationship with them, seduced by our own hormones to do *soul*-destructive things.

From this story, we begin to see how shame infiltrates our sexuality. Shame says we are dirty, we aren't enough, we are too much. Shame is a liar and the great kidnapper of healthy sexuality. Shame says we have to figure out life on our own. Being needy and not knowing is shame inducing for most. The serpent hijacked Adam and Eve by implying they were on their own and we humans have been trying to figure out our sexuality on our own ever since.

Because of this, we have made a tremendous mess of it all. We have done harm to ourselves and others. Thankfully, none of our mess is outside of His redemptive plan. With that said, we cannot be naive about how the Fall has sucked us into the vortex of shame—particularly shame about our sexuality. We learned from our first parents how to hide when we feel ashamed, how to put the fig leaves over our private parts and hope for the best. Our sexual brokenness began at the moment we could see evil and we separated our sexuality from our Creator in that moment.

CONSULTING OUR DESIGNER

My husband is a builder; together we have built seven homes. For each project we consult with our architect on a regular basis throughout the building process. Without consulting the designer we most likely would end up with something much less than what we originally hoped. The same is true for the development of our sexuality. Consulting with the Designer is our only hope that this significant part of ourselves, both personally and culturally, will find health.

I hope reading this story—God's love story of what was in His heart from the beginning, and how the story took a heart-wrenching turn—gives you a deeper understanding of why human sexuality has become so complex and is in desperate need of separating the good from the evil.

WHY IS LOVE IMPORTANT TO SEX?

Some believe sexuality was the devil's idea. I understand that thinking, given the horrendous ways we humans have used sexuality to manipulate, shame, control, harm, and overpower others. But clearly, sexuality was introduced before the Fall of mankind and our God is *the* God of Love. Simply stated, He is Love. He loves the world. And He invites us to love one another, saying it is the greatest thing we will ever do. We are to love others as we love ourselves. A relationship not growing in love will not be secure and solid. Love is a must. His word begins with a marriage in Genesis and finishes in grand finale with a marriage in Revelation, supporting the idea God made us for love relationships. God is in a sweet community of love and He invites us to create and participate with Him in loving relationships.

Our sexuality is intended to be grounded and rooted in God's love. He created mankind as one human being and then extracted the feminine from the masculine. They were originally one and sexual intercourse is the way in which the two become one again. God created sexual longing when He separated the two; instinctively, they long for the familiarity of the other's body and desire one another sexually. That God-given desire is a part of our makeup.

Being sexual with another human being was intended to be an expression of a love relationship. Scripture clearly makes a connection between married love and sex—a very necessary connection to make if we are going to reclaim the meaning and purpose of our sexuality. Some eliminate sex when they talk about love, thinking sexuality isn't holy enough to be connected to love, and others eliminate love when they talk about sex, believing sex is about lust. God wants us to have an integrated *wholeness* as we develop our ideas, thinking, and beliefs about human sexuality. He wants us to have a love map for the expression of our sexuality.

WHY IS IT IMPORTANT TO UNDERSTAND HOW OUR SEXUAL HISTORIES HAVE SHAPED US?

New brain science has proven we are wired for relationships during the first years of our lives. God's plan was for a child to be created by a loving husband who is committed to the well-being of his loving wife and she to him, so together they can commit to the well-being of their child. The mother has typically been the first love object of the newborn child and then the father is integrated as the child develops.

When Daddy and Mommy love one another well, together they can love the child well. The child is then securely attached and is wired for future love relationships. The child has learned the world is safe and people can be trusted. Those most significant caretakers are people by whom the child has been nurtured, soothed, and comforted. Snuggles, warmth, and empathy have been the foundation for this newborn's life.

Unfortunately, this isn't always the case. Many children are born into less than loving circumstances, some into cruel and evil environments. Instead of love wiring the child's brain for how he or she will think, act, and feel about future relationships, either anxiety about relationships or avoidance become the child's norm.

New Love Science (a work started in the 1960s by Dr. John Bowlby, a British psychologist and psychiatrist who developed the idea of attachment theory, which was continued by Dr. Sue Johnson and her colleagues) teaches us the necessity of attachment to form strong relationships. Dr. Johnson has applied Bowlby's theory of attachment to adult love relationships. Her research proves adults need attachment as desperately as do infants. I believe this aligns with God's plan for our lives. He created mankind to reflect Him, and He is in a community of love and support with the Father, Son, and Holy Spirit: three unique individuals with separate roles and yet one. Marriage is intended to be a reflection of this love triune with a husband, a wife, and God—husband, wife, and children—with love being the primary glue holding it all together.

How attachment went with our Family of Origin (FOO) is integral to understanding how we were shaped for love relationships.

In my own life, my mother could be warm and nurturing and available at times. Other times she was distant and unavailable. I later learned those were the times my father was either drinking heavily or acting out in some way. I formed a more anxious style of attaching because I was uncertain if I could count on my parents. Sometimes they were available, other times my father was stressed and highly reactive and downright frightening, and my mother was caught up in his behavior.

My husband came from a family of seven children, a daycare in his home, and foster children in and out. He was in the middle and learned to be more avoidant. Together, we have worked on our attachment styles to form a more solid, secure attachment. It hasn't happened easily or without tears, but every ounce of effort we have applied to learn how to turn toward each other instead of becoming either anxious or avoidant has been worth the secure love relationship we now share. At times, we still have some bumpy moments, but overall our attachment has grown strong and secure and is a great source of joy.

Sexuality is a significant part of our story, and our parents play a role in how we feel about our sexuality and what we do with it. If our parents had a healthy view of sexuality and were comfortable talking about sex, that shaped us in a positive way. If they were unhealthy and sex was a taboo topic in the house you grew up in, sex can be a really difficult topic.

If sex was treated without respect such as when porn was readily available, or off-handed sexual innuendos were tossed around, or parents were sexually unfaithful to one another, sexuality can seem dirty. If Mom and Dad modeled warmth, affection, and playful attraction, we learned our sexuality is something good. If our parents argued about sex, if one was cold and the other pouting because sex wasn't frequent enough, we learn sex is a power struggle. Either way, our parents are wiring our brain for future sexual relationships.

You may feel discouraged by this. Ron and I were at first as well. Neither set of our parents modeled healthy sexuality. There were lots of dark secrets to be sorted through. With God's help and the help of others, we can honestly say no sexual problem, no shameful secret, nothing you are hiding from is too impossible for God to heal.

THE FIRST TIME

Our first sexual encounter also forms our feelings and beliefs about sexuality. For some their first sexual encounter is loving, happy, and satisfying. Sadly, for too many, their first sexual encounter may not have been a positive experience. Yet, they are lasting experiences, and sometimes we find ourselves stuck in the memories, feelings, sensations, and images of those experiences.

Depending on the level and type of impression our first experiences make (from minor to traumatic) our wiring is again shaped and rewired. Neuroscience teaches us what gets fired together gets wired together. So if someone has a negative sexual experience, or interprets it as negative, the brain fires and then wires that memory into the circuitry.

Fortunately, God is the God of redemption and transformation. He wants every area of our lives to be made new in Christ Jesus. In order for that to happen, several things need to take place. We need to be sexually educated. We live in a sexually saturated society, but unfortunately, much of the saturation isn't positive, loving, or based on God's ideas for human sexuality.

Many people need a redo. We also need safe places with trustworthy people where our stories can be told. People need to be given permission to tell their stories to warm, loving individuals who will listen and not judge. The telling and retelling of significant stories allows our brains to make sense of, heal, and form a new ending to what may have been a very bad beginning.

WHY TELL A STORY?

Stories help us lower our defenses. Sometimes just the topic of sexuality can put our nervous system on high alert, depending on how we were raised, and what our early experiences were like. For example: If you were shamed for playing doctor, which is about childhood curiosity and signals to the parents the child needs more information about bodies and sexuality, shame can quickly become paired with sexual feelings.

Again, we are all sexual creatures with a sexual nervous system and if we are exposed to sexual stimuli, our bodies will respond. We aren't dreadful sinners, it's just the way we are wired. It's how God made us. When we can accept our sexuality as a natural part of who we are, we can accept ourselves and begin to rewire the broken parts.

I do believe God wants to help us connect our sexuality to our spirituality, and we can invite Him to be our teacher, guide, and helper. Sadly, because of shame, too many people hide their sexual selves from the eyes of the Creator instead of asking Him for help. We haven't strayed far from our original parents; Adam and Eve taught us well how to hide because we are afraid and because we feel naked (vulnerable) and ashamed.

But great sex is the fruit of doing the hard work, the soul work required to become a truly healthy self. The more you open your heart and invite the healing process in, the more likely you are to become and embrace the sexual creature you are. Willingly opening up your heart and mind to healing opens up new possibilities to play, explore, and have fun together sexually.

The more you do the work of healthy self-differentiation, the more connected you can become, and the more connected you are to yourself, God, and your spouse, the greater the potential for building erotic, sexual experiences together. Sex is ultimately about the condition of our hearts. If our hearts are closed down and shut off, that impacts how open we are to sharing our bodies with the one we chose to marry.

In order to demonstrate this truth, the following stories you are about to read are real stories (names, events, circumstances have all been changed to protect the identity of any one person). And through these stories, you will experience firsthand the effects of what evil has done to human sexuality and how God is the great Intervener in our lives, even the sexual part of our lives. I hope to create a dialogue for us to have a loving, shame-free, healing conversation about this most sacred and significant part of who we are. I invite you into the lives and vulnerabilities of the characters I have created to tell our shared experiences: how they found redemption and hope, and how you can as well. My purpose in telling stories is largely to make it safe for you to identify the areas of your sexuality in need of a redo. This book is for both males and females, married and single, young and old.

TWO

Real Life

Wherever you find yourself sexually, there is a story behind how you got there. God created your sexuality for a purpose, but you may wonder why. Why, God, when it can be so destructive? The reason sex is often so hurtful is because it is powerful. Sex is a metaphor for a God who wants an intimate, knowing relationship with each one of His children. Think how the enemy must hate this intimate part of God's purpose and how he wants to bring destruction to our sexuality. Your sexual history is a part of who you are. Instead of fearing it, be honest with yourself about your experiences, both positive and negative, and how those experiences have shaped and impacted you. Find safe relationships to sort it through, and ask for help if you need it. Your sexual wholeness is worth reclaiming.

MEET THE MEN

Kevin walked into the Texas frat house with his backpack slung over his LA-suntanned shoulder. His dimpled smile exuded confidence, but behind the sky-blue eyes lurked nagging insecurity. Kevin hid it well; few would ever notice. He spent too many hours in the gym toning his body, hoping the taut muscles and perfectly dressed physique would cover his hidden secret. He melted women with his playful smile and flirty eyes. He never lacked for a date or for friends, but deep inside he felt alone.

The first time he found his stepdad's stack of porn was when his mom was diagnosed with ovarian cancer. With his parents preoccupied with surgery, chemo, and radiation, he found the beautiful women posed on the glossy pages to be a strange sort of comfort. He felt warm and somehow accepted by the eyes penetrating his aloneness.

The weaker his mom became, the more he detached from her and attached himself to the glamorized, nude women. These women wouldn't leave him, he justified in his eight-year-old brain. Little did he know he was gradually shifting his need for human attachment onto a false image. The confusion of guilt feelings mixed with sexual arousal and the fear of losing his real mother puddled into the deep recesses of his brain, wiring this innocent little boy for a lifetime of sexual addiction struggles.

He was glad to leave Los Angeles behind—only bad memories lived there. He still blushed with disgust over his last date with Kate. Apparently, the years of masturbation and porn were dulling his ability to perform sexually. *Seriously,* he thought to himself, *How could someone like me have performance issues?*

His shoulder ready to rid itself of his overstuffed backpack, Kevin heaved it onto the ratty sofa in the frat common area. From the stairway, he spotted the largest human he had ever laid eyes on.

Jason was from the Midwest and the first to greet Kevin. He looked like a brick house. He was huge, all six feet six inches, three hundred pounds of him. He looked like a linebacker for some professional football team. Kevin soon learned that was exactly what Jason hoped he would become. He was highly pursued by the best universities in the country, but he made the final decision to come to Texas A&M on a full football scholarship. Kevin's first impression of Jason left no doubt in his mind that every goal Jason had he would achieve.

Kevin began to relax as Jason showed him around the house and made him feel at home. There was something down-to-earth about Jason that spawned a sensation in Kevin's gut. Was it trust? Kevin shook it off and flopped down on the edge of the bed Jason said was his.

Jason asked if he wanted to go check out the campus and find food. Always hungry, Kevin quickly agreed. While they wolfed down lunch, Kevin learned more about Jason. He was raised on a dairy farm in Nebraska, his mom and dad were still married, and he had five other siblings. He worked hard on the farm with his family, and though they didn't have much money, there was plenty of love to be shared. They gave him values, guidance, warmth, and security.

Jason mentioned church was a big part of his family's life. Kevin thought how unlike his family Jason's family was. After his mom died, Kevin went to live with his birth dad, who he hardly knew. His dad drank too much and Kevin basically raised himself. If it hadn't been for the care and kindness of his maternal grandmother, Kevin was sure he wouldn't still be alive.

While Kevin was toying with the idea he had just shared lunch with the most together guy on campus, Jason suddenly got real. He said, "It's good to be back at school, I sort of blew it last week with Grace." He went on to explain he had been dating Grace since their junior year of high school and they were engaged. She was the love of his life and the wedding was planned for spring break.

Kevin asked, "So what happened?"

"Well," Jason said, "I know this might sound really old fashioned to you, but I was raised to believe sex is for marriage. We love each other and on the last night, before I left to come back to school, we were kissing and things went a little too far. Everything in my body wanted her, and I could tell she felt the same way. We climbed into the back seat of my truck when boom it hit me what I was about to do. Luckily, my dad's voice and my mom's face came back into my head and well—that calmed things down. I was that close to taking her virginity, something I promised I wouldn't do until we were married and she was ready to give herself to me."

Kevin sat in silence and nodded, thinking how different he and Jason were.

Later that night Jeff and Trevor showed up blurry eyed from the long drive. They had been best friends since grade school. Jeff hoped a change of scenery might help his friend find his footing again. Trevor had been a disaster since tenth grade. Jeff watched as Trevor went from being a top student, captain of the

baseball team, and class president to smoking pot and not caring much what happened next. Jeff tried to get Trevor to talk to
him. He had a hunch that when his dad ran off with his new
girlfriend and his mom sank into depression it really messed
Trevor up.

Trevor spent most weekends at Jeff's house. His parents took
him under their wings, but Trevor wouldn't even open up to
them. He became emotionally numb and the pot seemed to help
him stay in denial. Jeff went from feeling concerned, to frustrated, to wanting to head-butt him. *Maybe this will help*, he
silently hoped.

Even though it was past midnight, all the lights were on in
the house and there was a mangy looking dog crawling out from
under the porch to greet them. Trevor wondered if he had fleas,
but decided he looked friendly enough to give him a pat.

The two-story house wasn't impressive—it smelt like leftover
pizza, stale beer, and looked like nobody's mother had been to
visit in the last three decades. Someone picked up the kitchen,
but it wasn't clean. A&M chairs filled in for furniture in the living room and what was once the kitchen table was filled with
week-old newspapers, coupon fliers, accounting books, and an
old pizza box with one piece of dried up pepperoni left. Jeff
looked hungrily at the box but decided to pass, wondering how
long it had been there. Trevor and Jeff stood in the living room,
their belongings lumped at their feet looking a little lost, when
Kevin came rumbling down the stairs.

"Hey guys!" He stuck out his hand and shook each of theirs.
Jeff looked him square in the eyes and gave him a firm hand-
shake. Trevor's was less convincing and he didn't completely

make eye contact. Kevin, raised in LA, knew that evasive look way too well. He sensed Trevor had a few secrets much like he did.

"Let me show you the *palace*," Kevin said as he rolled his eyes.

Later, a stillness settled over the house as the lights went out one by one. Kevin tossed in his bed as the familiar dream haunted his sleep. He was chasing after his mother, screaming for her in the dark, he was small, vulnerable, and alone. Aching penetrated each throb of his panicked heart. The cold sweat awakened him with a sudden realization he was not alone. He shared this room with Jason. Hot shame replaced his cold sweat.

The next morning Kevin rolled over relieved to see Jason's bed a crumpled, empty mess. Kevin wondered how someone that large slept comfortably in a twin bed. About that time, Jason showed up dripping from his morning run in the Texas heat.

"Hey," he said, "do you want to go to this thing with me today? It's a campus ministry that's a really big deal here, almost everyone goes, and you could meet most of the guys I hang out with."

"Um—sure—yeah, I guess." Later, Kevin convinced Jeff and Trevor to go with them.

Blaring from the coliseum was Tim McGraw's song, "Humble and Kind." Kevin thought that was interesting. The only time he attended anything religious was his grandmother's church, where they opened a musty hymnbook and sang songs from prehistoric times. He always pictured people wearing old western clothes, bonnets, and buns, with long skirts, and shirts buttoned to the neck. He loved the warmth of his grandmother and how she smelt like cookies, but her church made him fidget and pray to the God up there this would soon be over.

Kevin shook his head to awaken himself to the present. Texas wasn't anything like LA. People shook his hand with a friendliness and directness he wasn't used to. He noticed how both guys and good-looking girls with bleach-blonde hair, and long, Texastanned legs, flocked to Jason. He was a sort of hero. Kevin liked being his new roommate and wondered how weird it was that he, the lost kid from LA, was here with this giant of a man. He looked over at Jeff and Trevor and saw the same mystified look on their faces.

The band played three more songs that pricked at him; he looked around, and some of the students had their eyes closed and hands raised. Again, he shook his head and wondered where he was. About that time, a guy who looked like he was in his mid-thirties thanked the band and prayed. He prayed in a way that seemed more like a conversation than repeating words to someone far, far away. He said his name was James.

James looked at the students filling the brightly lit room. He said, "Welcome to Real Life. I'm your campus pastor. My wife and I are here for you. Kaycie, would you come up here and bring the boys with you?"

His wife gathered their three little boys, as she walked to the platform. Her long, red hair was a contrast to most of the blondes in attendance. She was stunning, with soft blue-gray eyes, and was gentle with her three rowdy sons. She put her arm around James's waist and gave him a warm smile. For the second time since he arrived at Texas A&M, Kevin felt something warm in his gut. *Was it a longing? Trust?* Again, he brushed the feeling aside to focus on what James was saying after Kaycie and their three little boys rumbled off the platform.

James said, "Sometime this year Kaycie will share her story with you. I promise you don't want to miss what she has to say. My wife is my hero. We have been through some hard times, and we hope our story can help you avoid some of our mistakes. This is Real Life. We don't pull punches here. We aren't religious, but we do love Jesus and believe He is alive and real and wants to help each of us do real life. We talk about the issues relevant to college students. So let's get started.

"If you want to turn to the passage I am speaking from, open the Bible app on your smartphone to 1 Thessalonians 4. You might think this is a weird place to begin considering the Apostle Paul starts with, 'One final word, friends.' But I love how Paul just gets right to it and since I am a Texas boy I like getting right into it too." Then he read:

> We ask you—urge is more like it—that you keep on doing what we told you to do to please God, not in a dogged religious plod, but in a living, spirited dance. You know the guidelines we laid out for you from the Master Jesus. God wants you to live a pure life. Keep yourselves from sexual promiscuity. Learn to appreciate and give dignity to your body, not abusing it, as is so common among those who know nothing of God (1 Thess. 4:1–5).

"Man, I wish I'd known something about this kind of a life. You may think Kaycie and I have it all together. The truth is the first time we met was in a dark basement at a frat party. We sat across from a coffee table splattered with beer bottles, pot, and cocaine. We shared a line of cocaine, got high, and slept together for the first time without hardly sharing a word or knowing each other's last names. We were so lost we didn't know up from down, and we sure didn't give dignity to our bodies. Instead, we abused our bodies and took from each other what we thought would remove the empty, lonely pit we found ourselves in.

"If that wasn't enough, I was also addicted to porn and Kaycie—well, she will tell you her own story. A month before graduation, Kaycie discovered she was pregnant. That little red-haired guy, yeah, he was the result of our college days. Don't get me wrong; I love Sam. He's a gift and a big part of why we both got sober. We have needed a lot of help. The hardest part and the one with the strongest grip on my mind was the porn. My older brother introduced me to it, and before I knew it, I started planning my days around losing myself in what I once thought was the best drug I ever discovered. It was my dirty little secret. I thought it hurt no one until two months after Sam was born, Kaycie found me late one night indulging in my private life.

"It was humiliating, so I tried to put it off on her and the new baby. After all, I justified, we weren't exactly having a ton of sex since she got pregnant and had the baby. It wasn't until I got help that I realized how completely selfish I was and how my secret was hurting the people I loved.

"I know I'm not alone. College can seem like a time to spread your wings and get free from your high school days or maybe your parents' rules. I get that. Nobody wanted his or her freedom more than me. My dad was a preacher and I had my bellyful of religion and rules by the time I got to college. You may be shocked I am talking so openly about sex, drugs, and religion, but these are the big issues you are going to face in the next several years. You will make choices that will impact the rest of your lives.

"Kaycie and I have walked this journey out. It has been messy and at times heartbreaking. We have hurt each other, our families, and ourselves. But we have also experienced grace, compassion, forgiveness, and a new way of doing life. We have committed our lives to helping you do the same, if that's what you want. *No secrets.*

"Open, honest, real-life conversations and dialogues are welcome here. We don't want to pretend we have all the answers. We don't. We are still learning and discovering. But this we do know: God is for you, and He will not leave you even when you are at your worst. And neither will we.

"Jesus wants a relationship with you. It's a relationship with Jesus that changed my life. I'm so grateful He found me in my darkest days. I grew up in the church; I was there every time the doors were open, and I went up front every summer at youth camp to give my life to Jesus, but a week later, I took it back. I thought my dad represented God, and if God was as mean as my dad, then I didn't want anything to do with him.

"My dad would preach on Sunday and whip me for fun later the same day. The gospel became very twisted inside me. God loves me, and my dad loves God, but my dad was as mean as a snake, and I personally thought he was the devil. When I heard the way he yelled at my mom, the thuds I heard coming from their bedroom, and her quiet whimpers and bruises in the morning, it made me hate him more. When I left for college, I didn't want anything to do with God or Jesus His son.

"I came to A&M running away from it all and believing I could leave that life behind. But the nightmares and memories didn't leave me so I started using porn and drinking. That worked for two years to numb the pain inside me. When it stopped working, I tried something stronger and when I found myself needing more and more to get the same high, I knew I needed help. Honestly, I had no clue where to find help. The church only told me what was wrong with me.

"Thankfully, I had a roommate who never gave up on me. He was a solid guy from a solid family. I respected him and he was one of the few people I trusted. He asked me if I would come to Real Life with him and what seemed completely random ended up being the best decision of my life. I found real people who didn't shame me because I was a mess. They loved me through my mess, took time to have a relationship with me, and showed me the love of God in a real way.

"Several of the Real Life leaders shared how trauma played a big part in the role of porn, alcohol, and drugs. They had a specialist come in who taught us about how our brain was wired and how I used porn to try to dull the hurt inside me and release *feel-good* chemicals. I wanted to temporarily stop the pain and soothe myself. They didn't shun me or shame me, but instead taught me about how neurochemistry, thought processes, my family, and spiritual interactions affected my brain functions. They even taught me praying more and trying harder would not change my addictive behaviors. These guys stuck with me when I felt unlovable and undeserving of their friendship.

"I can't express how grateful I am for my healing journey. I will freely admit that sometimes I wanted to quit, give up, and walk away. But the love and healthy intimacy Kaycie and I now share made the journey worth it.

"Enough about my story and me. I don't know your story, but I want to. I honestly hope your story is different than mine, but if it's not, I want you to know it's okay. I have posted my calendar on the screen, my number, and the hours I have available to meet with you. You will see Kaycie's number and hours there as well. We also have a staff and we all live by the same belief. Real Life—we wouldn't have it any other way."

With that, he closed his eyes and prayed. He dismissed the students, as music blared from the band. Jason turned to Kevin, Trevor, and Jeff and asked what they thought. They simultaneously shrugged their shoulders trying to find words.

Kevin spoke first, "I can relate. His story is different than mine, but similar. I might like this guy; hey, I might come back with you."

"Me too," Jeff said.

Trevor just nodded, giving neither a yes or no.

FINAL THOUGHT

In this first chapter, you have been introduced to our four college guys and James. Maybe you are not relating to one in particular yet, but I believe if you keep reading you will identify with someone. Not everyone's sexual lives get as complex as Kevin's and James's; some couples just suffer from sexual boredom or apathy. Nonetheless, my belief is wherever you find yourself sexually there is a story behind how you got there. For those of you who struggle with addiction, it's helpful to know most addicts begin life as sensitive truth tellers who later hide, numb, and pretend, because life seems too painful.

Take a few minutes and locate yourself. Where are you sexually? Are you in a healthy place? A broken place? A place you don't want to be? Maybe you could grab your journal and jot down a few thoughts and emotions as you begin to unpack your own sexual history.

THREE

The Secret

Every woman has a sexual history, and every woman can carry false guilt about her sexuality or shame about herself as a sexual creature. Sometimes, just the topic of sexuality can put our nervous systems on high alert, depending on how we were raised and our early experiences. However, I would like to help you uncover your story. Stories are truly a powerful thing and when we can tell our story and bring our secrets into the light, we can rewrite our ending. I want to give you permission to not only tell your story, unearth your past, and grieve your losses, but also to discover, claim, and own the fullness of the unique expression of your sexual self.

It may surprise you to know women are as sexual as men; they just have a different pathway for getting there. Female sexuality looks different from male sexuality and there is no shame in that. We will never get to the fun part of discovering our sexual selves if we are buried under shame, self-hatred, and secrets. Secrets are suffocating to their keepers, and the only way to begin a true sexual journey of freedom is to unearth that which is hidden.

In order to be healthy sexually, we have to be committed to the personal growth process, which in truth is a journey that begins in the form of story, your story. It doesn't matter where you are or what you have experienced—it matters where you are going. If you choose to move toward embracing your healthy sexual self, understand this is not a "take a few numbered steps and you're done" process. No, this truly is a journey. But like any journey, you have to start somewhere, so start with you. Start by being honest with yourself about your sexual past and give yourself permission not to minimize your experiences and the effect your history has had on you.

It was never God's intent for us to do life alone. Your personal growth process requires courage. But know it's okay to ask for help and even to need help, as you will discover Kaycie did. Kaycie needed help to uncover a dark secret that was sabotaging her sexual health and her marital intimacy. So let's travel back three years earlier to when Kaycie's story unfolds.

THREE YEARS EARLIER

Kaycie woke early, grateful she had an appointment with the therapist she had been seeing for the last six months. Once James sorted through his sexual past and the fog began to clear from their marriage, she could see how her own past was interfering with the two of them sharing true intimacy.

She found herself avoiding his initiations with one lame excuse after another, usually to do with the kids needing her for something. This morning, she felt the wall she was building to keep James away growing taller. She knew this wasn't what she wanted, but something inside her pushed against him anyway.

Kaycie rolled over and watched James sleeping. She loved how peaceful he looked and soaked in his tanned, lean muscles from years of running in the Texas sun. Fondness swept over her, followed too quickly by the memory of him cheating on her. Suddenly the current of bad memories washed away the warmth and love she was experiencing.

Frustrated, she grabbed her robe and headed to the bathroom. *Why*, she pondered, couldn't she just stay with the new, good memories? Give James a chance to be the new man she believed he was becoming? The Bible talks about the old becoming new and how in Christ we are a new creation. Instead of feeling angry with James, she felt disgusted with herself. Talking to the reflection in the mirror, Kaycie said, "Maybe you aren't a very good Christian. You need to get your act together and try harder to forgive and love this man."

With the baby crying in the back seat, Kaycie was relieved when she dropped Sam at school. She was even more relieved to get her younger two boys situated with her mom. While in the waiting room of her counselor's office, she fidgeted with the bracelet James gave her for her thirty-first birthday. Engraved were the words, "Two are better than one." Hmm—she wondered if it was true for them.

She stared out the window, exploring how two people who hurt each other so deeply could ever heal and move forward. It seemed easier for James to let go, but then again, she reasoned, she wasn't the one who cheated. A chill ran down her spine with the recollection of learning, not only was there a porn issue, but once he was six months into recovery he confessed that early in their marriage he had a one-night stand. Ouch! The memory still stung.

Kaycie was grateful for the interruption when the waiting-room door swung open. The familiar smile of her therapist shook her brain out of the negative rehearsal. She dumped her over-loaded purse filled with baby wipes, crackers, and gummy bears at her feet and settled into the familiar sofa. Olivia's smile always calmed her and reassured Kaycie she wasn't some hopeless freak.

"Kaycie, where would you like to start today?"

Kaycie took a deep breath and heard herself exhale before she said, "It's not all James. The healthier he gets, the more I can see my own issues. I want to work on me. I have faced and grieved the one-night stand and the porn issues, but I think I need to take the focus off of James—it keeps me stuck in the past and avoiding my own issues. I need your help to move forward."

"Kaycie," Olivia looked at her with a twinkle in her eye, "I have been hoping you would come to this place. You have done the hard work of facing the marital issues, and I am celebrating that you are ready to face your own. Besides, a healthy marriage consists of two individuals who are doing the hard work of healing their own souls. So let me ask, where would you like to start working on you?"

Kaycie nervously clutched her hands in her lap, "Well, James and I have a theme with the students, "No secrets," but to be honest, I have never shared with anyone my biggest secret. And I'm not sure I have told myself…"

Kaycie stiffened as a red rash crept up her chest and onto her neck. "My senior year of high school, I had two youth pastors. One was incredible; he was round-faced with a warm, dimpled smile. He adored his wife and four little boys. He was completely dedicated to the youth group. He loved God and really wanted the best for all of us. I trusted him."

Olivia nodded and leaned in knowing there was more.

"There was another youth pastor. He was all about himself, he needed to be a big deal and do big things to make himself look good. He frequently invited me to come to his office and sometimes he would talk to me about sexual things. I felt really uncomfortable and didn't know what to do so I just tried to create distance from him. Several times he touched me on the shoulder in a way that gave me the creeps. On a youth retreat deep in the mountains of Washington, he asked me to go for a walk with him. I refused over and over, but he would not hear my no. He was insistent, saying he needed to talk to me about some leadership position he wanted me to fulfill. With my heart sinking and a sick feeling in my stomach, I just couldn't see a way out of it. Reluctantly, I shrugged my shoulders and relented. As we walked, he immediately started badgering me about why I was so different from all of the other girls. He said they all wanted him sexually and there was something wrong with me because I didn't appreciate his advances. I felt frozen as he pushed me to the ground and..." A dead terror filled Kaycie's eyes as she sat frozen.

Olivia moved from her leather chair to sit at Kaycie's feet. "May I put my hands on your feet to ground you?" she asked.

Kaycie nodded in the affirmative.

Olivia said, "Kaycie, you are here with me. What color are my eyes?"

Kaycie reconnected with the present and said, "They are blue with some soft green and gray."

"What is your favorite flower?"

Kaycie, a little puzzled, said, "I love blue hydrangeas."

Olivia, satisfied Kaycie wasn't regressing, asked gently, "Can you tell me more about your story?"

Kaycie inhaled sharply and continued, her voice shaking with emotion, "He slapped me, pushed me to the ground, climbed on top of me, and…"

"And what Kaycie?"

"He raped me." At that Kaycie let out a sob, followed by another and then another and then another.

"Yes, Kaycie, let it out. You have carried this for so long and it wasn't your fault. It wasn't your fault, Kaycie. He committed a crime against you, and it's time for you to grieve what was stolen from you."

Kaycie wept—the years of shame she carried, the loss, the grief, the embarrassment, the secret—it all came tumbling out.

The hour was nearing as Kaycie quieted. She was like a child spent.

The compassion she saw in Olivia's tearful eyes gave her a peace she hadn't experienced since the rape. The fear Olivia would see her differently wasn't there. She felt heard, understood, and known.

Olivia wrapped up the session by saying, "Kaycie, what happened to you was traumatic. I hurt with you over your loss. Telling your story is the beginning to your healing, as is grieving your story. Letting the pain out is significant. Rape affects a woman in so many ways; loss of confidence and self-esteem, shame taking root, depression setting in, loss of what once brought her joy, and shutting down or acting out sexually are all symptoms of a sexual assault. Some women develop self-hatred and blame themselves for what happened. You may have even wondered why you have carried around depression like a low-grade fever, sometimes struggling to just get out of bed in the morning can feel like a feat."

"Kaycie, you will have more to process around what happened, but today was a big start. On a practical note; drink lots of water to flush out the emotional toxins, and make sure you eat some protein. Self-care in the next few days will be important. Love yourself well and give yourself permission to be kind to you. You may have a shame hangover later for letting the secret out. Please tell that shame to leave you alone and to shut up. It took tremendous courage to tell your secret, and I am proud of you. Ask James for what you need. Do you have any questions?"

Kaycie nodded. "Yeah, what's a shame hangover?"

Olivia replied, "Well, it's a term I use to describe how people often feel after they let out a big truth, especially a secret that involves shame. And let's face it a sexual assault is wrapped in shame. Kaycie, the shame wasn't yours. The shame actually belongs to the youth pastor who raped you. But when someone uses your body for their own purposes, often shame is transferred and picked up by the victim. We will work on giving it back to him, but that will most likely be a process. Does that make sense?"

"Yes, I think so," Kaycie answered. "I have experienced a shame hangover before, I just never had a term for it. I think the hardest part is knowing how I should talk to myself when I have a shame hangover."

"Great point, Kaycie. With our self-talk we can either validate and give shame a greater hold on our lives, or we have the power to disarm shame. We disarm shame by telling ourselves the truth mixed with loads of grace. So what might it sound like for you to disarm shame with your self-talk?"

"Well—I guess I could tell shame it wasn't my fault, and I have nothing to be ashamed about. I didn't do anything wrong; he did. It isn't my shame—it belongs to him."

"Yes," Olivia affirmed. "How does it feel to voice that, Kaycie?"

"Empowering," Kaycie quickly answered.

Olivia continued. "You have processed a lot today. We will pick back up right here next week, so what we did here today we will revisit. Your brain is trying to make sense of what happened to you, and we have to let this be a healing journey."

Kaycie looked Olivia in the eyes, grateful for someone safe in her life to practice telling her truth to. Relieved, she gathered her purse and stuffed the pile of wet tissues into the side pocket. She sat in her car for a long time noticing her own feelings. She wondered why it took so long for her to tell her story. And it dawned on her that the rape may have impacted her in ways she never connected.

Kaycie recalled life before the rape and how she loved school, friends, cheerleading, skiing, and her dog. After the rape, life went dark, and the color drained out of her world. Gone were the simple joys of cold air on her cheeks and the smile of a friend.

Instead, she started drinking to numb the pain and she slept with
her boyfriend; after all, she reasoned, her virginity, something
she had hoped to save for her husband, was stolen.

Kaycie hoped leaving her small hometown behind would give
her a fresh start. Unfortunately, the secret, tightly packed away
in the recesses of her heart, travelled with her. Wine became her
ruby-red companion, helping her sleep, forget, and remain numb
enough to fake her way through life. It wasn't until her junior
year and wanting to garner the attention of James that she
snorted her first line of cocaine. This high sailed her to new
heights, but the low sank her soul into a darkness she had never
known. Now, she had a new understanding of why James's and
her marriage had been such a disaster. What they both brought
to the table was, to say the least, messy.

Kaycie straightened her shoulders, let out a deep breath,
and felt hope, as she started the car and pulled out of the parking lot. *Real life,* she pondered when she pulled up to her mom's
house, was better than a numb, empty, secret-keeping life. As
she walked up the concrete pathway to her mom's ranch style
home, she noticed she felt lighter. Maybe Olivia was right—
grieving does recalibrate your soul. When Kaycie first started
counseling, Olivia tried to encourage Kaycie to grieve her
losses. Olivia could tell Kaycie was carrying a lot of baggage.
But always, Kaycie would look at her like she was an alien
speaking a foreign language, "What good will grieving do? I
have cried. I have felt sorry for myself. And it hasn't helped so
far," she said.

Olivia would patiently nod and say, "I understand, Kaycie,
but I think grief is different than just tears. It does include tears,

but it also includes coming face to face with the reality of what has happened in your life and to you."

Kaycie learned to grieve what happened between her and James. And it helped tremendously, but Kaycie resisted applying grief to her own secrets. After today, Kaycie understood why she needed to tell her story—it made it real. She realized she never grieved for herself because she neglected to tell herself the truth. She recalled a Bible passage that said something like, *The truth will set you free.* Truth—I told the truth today, and I do feel something— maybe the rumblings of freedom? Relief? Hope? Whatever it is—I like it. Kaycie silently mused.

Later that night, after the mayhem of dinner, dishes, baths, and bedtime stories with kisses and hugs and one more sip of water, the house was quiet. James made Kaycie a cup of chamomile tea and invited her to sit outside under the stars for a few minutes together.

Kaycie froze for a second. Since James began his recovery process, he longed for genuine conversations and regularly invited Kaycie to open up to him. Yet, with each invitation, Kaycie's first instinct was to shut down and hide. But tonight Kaycie felt different. The day had changed her. She reasoned with herself she had something real to say and she wanted to say it.

She squared her shoulders as she followed him out to the back patio. They sat quietly for a few moments, each gazing up at the black sky with stars twinkling their happy hellos. Kaycie felt her tense shoulders relax and she moved to snuggle into James's open left arm. He cradled her and the connection growing between them calmed her nerves.

"James, I have a secret to tell you," she stated nervously. "And I am scared to tell you. I have kept something from you that you have a right to know, and now I am afraid if I tell you, you might be angry and reject me. It's not fair for me to ask you not to get angry, but I really need you not to get angry. Please."

"Kaycie, how many of my secrets have you had to face? And you haven't left me, which, honestly—I still can't figure out why you have been so gracious to me. I pray I can do the same for you—it's the least I can do," James gently reassured, pulling her in closer and kissing her forehead. He continued, "Kaycie, I love you and we both know what secrets have done to us. Now, I want to be a safe harbor for you to come home to. It's okay to tell me."

With that, Kaycie pulled away, sat up straight, and looked James in the eyes. Her chest felt tight with emotion, but she knew she had to press on. "My senior year of high school," her voice trailed off.

"Go on. I'm listening," James reassured his wife.

"My youth pastor—not the good one, the other one—he badgered me to go for a walk with him when we were at a youth retreat. Instinctively, I said no, but he wouldn't hear my refusal, even though I said it at least five times. I felt trapped and scared—frozen. I couldn't think of a way out of it. So, finally, I relented. He immediately started to harass me, completely throwing me off guard emotionally, telling me how weird I was. He wanted to know why I wasn't like the other girls who all wanted him sexually. I tried to explain to him that I had a boyfriend my own age, and he was married, and it was just wrong.

"Suddenly, he slapped me and pushed me to the ground. Next, he was on top of me and well...for years the rest was a blur. The next thing I knew, I was in the girls' bathroom at the lodge, crying hysterically with my girl friends gathered around me trying to console me. I don't even know how I got there. I don't know what happened afterward either. James, I would remember little bits and pieces, but I could never put together the whole story until today with Olivia. I have been having dreams— more like nightmares—at night. Since I started counseling, I always pray the night before I go to see Olivia that God will reveal what needs to heal. Well, I finally remembered the rest of the story. What happened when he knocked me to the ground— James..." She paused before she said, "He raped me. There, I said it. I have told you what a jerk he was and how he would put the move on me, but I never told you he raped me. But he did and that is the secret I have kept from you."

For a moment James looked like he had been slapped. "That bastard! I want to kill him!" he said, as he jumped up from the patio sofa, pounding his fists together. Then he caught himself, took a deep breath and collected his senses, sat back down, and said, "Kaycie, I am so sorry. No man should have ever done that to you; I can't imagine how terrifying, confusing, and hard that was for you. I wish I could have been there to protect you. You deserved to be protected. It wasn't your fault. It wasn't your fault..."

Tears appeared in James's eyes, as he reached to wipe the ones falling from Kaycie's. He gathered Kaycie into his arms and held her as they grieved. Silence gave her story the honor it deserved. Silence, tears, sorrow—and how a rape her senior year of high school stole from the woman he loved, stole from him, and stole joy from their marriage.

Tears spent, James reminded Kaycie of how deeply he loved and admired her. He said, "Kaycie, you are so brave. Thank you for having the guts to tell me your secret. I feel closer to you. I promise to hold it right here," as he patted his heart. "It's safe with me," James continued. "Your telling me makes me want to love you better, to be more compassionate and tender with you. Help me love you through this, would you?"

Kaycie was so relieved James hadn't reacted like the old James would have. Smiling, she said, "Yeah, I would be happy to let you love me through this. I think a wall came down today or at least a few bricks were removed—I want to let your love in. I know it's there, but I have been strong-arming you. Help me let your love in." Her words were framed with the emotional connection only honesty brings.

James carried Kaycie's now cold mug of tea into the kitchen. Relief filled the air, as they quietly prepared for bed. James, always ready first, lay in bed with his hands folded under his head, pondering how long he had been hoping, praying his wife would open up to him.

Shaking him from his thoughts, Kaycie quietly stood naked beside the bed. James looked her solidly in the eyes, as he reached for her hand. Searching her face, he saw desire there instead of duty or resentment. He lifted the covers, as his eyes invited her close. This time, the first time in a long, long time, Kaycie responded to his invitation. *Maybe two are better than one,* she thought, as she laid her head on his chest and wrapped her legs around his.

His body next to hers felt warm and safe. James remained still, soaking in the moment. He silently prayed for healing over his wife and healing for the sexual part of their relationship. A new compassion flooded his senses; never again did he want to anxiously take sexually from his wife. Instead, he prayed God would teach him how to really love her. He just held her until they both fell peacefully asleep.

FINAL THOUGHTS

I want to normalize what you might be feeling right now. You may be feeling some strong emotions. You may have tears in your eyes or a tightness in your chest. If you have experienced something like Kaycie did, you may feel vulnerable or have feelings of disgust about what happened. You most likely need containment (to be anchored). It's okay; even though this doesn't feel normal, you are normal to have these feelings. Many people experience unwanted sexual touch and, if they choose to engage in the healing process, healing can begin.

So let's ponder some questions together. Take a few minutes to write down your answers to these questions. Brain science teaches us that writing heals one part of our brain and talking heals the other. Let's begin your healing journey right now.

1. Can you identify with Kaycie's story in any way?
2. Have you ever experienced any unwanted sexual touch?
3. Have you told your story to a safe, loving person?
4. Have you given yourself permission to grieve your loss?

5. What do you need to heal?

Did you know God hates that you were touched in an unsafe and unwanted way? This was never His will for your life. Sadly, people can do some pretty cruel things to one another. Jesus came to this earth to heal the brokenhearted and to set the captive free (Isaiah 61). He is near the hurting and promises to never leave you. He brings comfort to those who grieve. Let Him draw near to you right now. He is not ashamed of you or your story.

Honestly, God says in His word that bad things will happen because we live in a fallen, broken world. Too often we blame Him for those bad things, when in reality it is humans who make the hurtful choices. He loves you, is for you, gave up His Son for your healing, and sent the comforter, the Holy Spirit to be with you. He will never ask you to do something and then leave you alone to do it. If you invite Him to join you on this journey, He happily will.

However, you may be thinking, *I'm the person who touched somebody in a way they didn't want. Is there hope for me?* If this is you, then you need to engage in the healing process as well. You will need to explore what happened in your past that caused or contributed to your behavior.

1. Was there any sexual abuse in your history?
2. Did anyone model taking from or being aggressive toward another human being as okay?
3. Is porn a contributing factor?
4. Are there any secrets you are holding?
5. What is considered normal sexual behavior in your family or friendships?

OWNING IT

Confession will be a significant part of your journey. Taking full responsibility for what you did is valuable and necessary. James 5:16 reads, "Therefore confess your sins to each other and pray for each other so that you may be healed. The prayer of a righteous person is powerful and effective" (NLT). Confession is powerful and serves as a washing.

Confession also allows you to evaluate if any repair work needs to be done. Repair work requires you to walk through a process of personal healing and growth; you take full responsibility for what you did, and if you need to make amends, you can then make amends. We can't fix what has already been done, but we can do our part in the healing process. It may include writing a letter to the person you hurt or talking to the person face-to-face if the victim feels safe enough to talk with you. If amends aren't possible, I would still encourage you to write out a letter, taking full responsibility, and reading it to a mentor, friend, or therapist.

I know this may feel overwhelming to even think about. And most likely your brain may have gone into a state of fight, flight, or freeze. That is because our amygdala is fear-central and we store our memories there. So, I want to normalize that if you are feeling argumentative or defensive—"No! That didn't happen to me," or "No, it was no big deal,"—where you are *minimizing* or *in denial*, I get that. You may just want to get up right now and run, or just "unzip your skin" and get out of your own self, or you might just want to shut down. I understand that, and those are common responses. You are normal. But God wants to heal your heart and your brain. Every healing journey begins by being honest about what happened. It wasn't your fault, but even if you did something that was your fault, nothing is outside the reaches of God's redemptive healing power.

So here are a few thoughts that I would like to leave with you, as you are moving forward on your sexual journey.

MOVING FORWARD

1. Break your denial structure by telling your story to a safe person or therapist. Practice with a little story first and see how they respond. Some might surprise you and some might disappoint you, but realize it is all part of the healing journey. *Be willing to let someone surprise you.*

2. You were wounded in a relationship, but you have to get some safe relationships around you in order to heal. Healing does not happen in isolation. Bring your pain into community. But you might need to test the waters to see who is safe.

3. Know God wants to heal you, and He is for you. So invite Him in. Ask God to reveal what needs to be healed and allow Him to do His good work in you.

4. Give yourself permission to grieve, but don't do it alone. Don't spend weeks crying by yourself with the covers over your head. You have lived through the worst of it. You are a survivor—now comes the healing part. Bring your story into community with God and others.

FOUR

Love and Longing

Before we can understand how a person has become who they are, we must first understand their history. I am always thankful God sees the beginning, the middle, and the end of our lives and has so much grace for our stories. In this chapter, we will process sexual addiction and confusion, but before we get into the story, here is some helpful information.

Sexual addictions—where do they come from? The answer may surprise you. Studies reveal 60–70 percent of men and 20–30 percent of women struggle with sexual addiction.[1] And sexual addiction isn't about sex—it's about medicating pain. Sexual addictions often go untreated because of shame. Shame is the great silencer and isolator. Men and women struggling with sexual issues often feel so shameful they continue to struggle alone. They have a personal shame perspective—afraid they would be judged and ostracized if others knew the trap in which they are caught.

What we need to understand is sexual addiction often has roots in wounds. Many have experienced family dysfunction or personal trauma, and come from a culture of addictions. Often, there is a history of a binge-purge cycle, sober for a while and then back at it full blast. They typically live in denial about how bad the problem is and believe if they try harder all will be well.

In this next chapter, we will be following Trevor, who we discover suffers from sexual confusion and struggles with using porn. Because of relational difficulties with his father, Trevor has never attached to his dad or to a healthy male role model. Trevor's dad, Keith, chose rules over a relationship with Trevor. He was also avoidant in his attachment style, fearful of being close to another human being.

A child is designed to attach to both of his or her parents. Infants need the warmth, snuggling, cuddling, and closeness of a caregiver. As the child develops, it's so important for the child to identify with their same-sex parent; and when attachment takes place, the parent can be a role model to their child, showing them how to do life as either a male or female. But, if attachment does not take place, or when the child is repulsed by their same-sex parent, the child may be more prone to struggle with sexual and identity issues.

Of course, we can never say always or never when it comes to understanding human sexuality. Humans are all unique and I am not attempting to say this is true of all people, but this is Trevor's story and what was true for him. However, others who struggle with sexual issues might have fond memories of attachment and remember receiving warmth and comfort from their parents. I do not want to be guilty of blaming parents for their children's sexual choices. Truthfully, research has not uncovered definitive answers as to what causes same-sex attraction. What I am attempting to do is to create a more compassionate understanding for those who do struggle.

When a child is nurtured by a warm and loving parent, they are given security; they experience a secure sense of self and a healthy view of who they are in this world as a male or female. Children need a warm, loving parent to interact with them. Fathers are meant to wrestle with their kids and physically give their child a sense of body confidence. Healthy attachment for a child helps answer the questions deep within them such as: Who am I as a male or female in this world? Where do I fit in? How do I feel about my gender, my masculinity or femininity?

THE POWER OF THE FOO

Family of Origin (FOO) wounds affect our sexuality. When a family is dysfunctional, children internalize the dysfunction and develop attachment wounds. Many become either avoidant, realizing attachment is unsafe, or they become anxious about attachment and fear a loss of connection, making them prone to codependency and addictions. For this person, sex becomes a substitute for genuine love and attachment. Beliefs are then hardwired into their neurochemistry: I'm not good enough; there is something wrong with me; I am bad; I'm worthless; I am not worthy of attachment.

Adopted as a child, Trevor has never bonded with his same-sex parent. Trevor's father was a role model for the type of person Trevor doesn't want to be; and Trevor perceives his father as being unkind, unfaithful, undependable, and unavailable. Thus, Trevor feels like he doesn't want to be the type of male his father is, but what type of male does he want to be? The lack of attachment to his father and the lack of a guiding role model leaves Trevor feeling confused about his identity and his sexuality. So how does this look in the life of a young man who just wants to be loved and to feel connected?

THE BEGINNING

Trevor was roused from a deep sleep by voices in the living room. He rolled his small six-year-old frame out of his twin bed and followed the angry sounds, as he rubbed the sleep from his brown eyes. His mom gripped her robe, wrapping it tightly around her shaking body, as if the soft pink fabric was a coat of armor. His dad, Keith, stood over her with his fists clenched and the veins in his neck popping. When his dad saw him, he launched at Trevor, but his mom was quick, stepping between the two of them.

His dad said with a sneer, "Hiding behind your mom, what a wuss you are and always will be! Such a disappointment for a son." With that, his dad stormed out of the house, squealing the tires of his sports car as he drove off. Trevor thought about the neighbors in their middle-class homes awakening to the sound of doors slamming and tires spewing rocks instead of the beeping of their alarm clocks.

His attention quickly refocused from the neighbors to his mother sitting on the beige sofa crying. He went to comfort her.

"Mom," he assured her, "we can make it without him. We don't need him; I can take care of you." The six-year-old believed every word he said to his emotionally battered and fragile mother. He was too young to know what was involved in supporting a household and yet emotionally old enough to feel the burden and responsibility of taking care of his mother. He never doubted his mother's love for him, but being her surrogate husband was heavy—love was heavy and burdensome. He felt the responsibility for her happiness and he wanted to make her miserable life better by being everything she could hope for. He determined to make her life worth living. He would give her someone to be proud of and fill her unhappy life with a little joy.

He wrapped his arms around her, until she stopped crying. He then went to the kitchen and turned the tea kettle on, knowing tea always made his mom feel better. He got out the box of Honey Nut Cheerios and poured himself a bowl. Eat, get dressed, brush teeth, and get himself to school became his immediate goal. School was his refuge and a place where he could make his mom proud.

It was the next right thing to do. After all, he was a good little soldier. No time for his tears, or sadness that his father was a bully and his mother was emotionally weak. No one to process what his needs might be after his father called him a disappointment. The word reverberated somewhere deep inside his chest. He wasn't sure what the word meant, but he had a complete understanding it was a word that held meaning and already had begun to define how Trevor perceived himself.

On the walk to school, with low-lying, gray clouds overhead to match his mood, Trevor hardly noticed the wind against his cold cheeks. He continually replayed in his mind the words his father spoke. They circled around inside of his six-year-old brain until they found a place to connect and wire permanently into his moldable belief system about who he was as a male.

He loved his teacher, Mrs. Hampton. She noticed him and she smelled like vanilla. He loved that smell; it reminded him of when his mom made sugar cookies for him.

"Trevor," she said softly, as she walked up and down the rows, pausing momentarily at his desk, "stay in here during recess. I want to talk with you. You aren't in trouble; I just want to make sure you are okay." She asked another student, Johnny, to stay in as well.

When the other kids scampered out of the classroom, noisily excited for a breath of freedom, Mrs. Hampton landed her warm eyes on Trevor and Johnny.

"Hey, you both seem a little sad today. Is everything okay at home?"

Johnny looked at Trevor and then spoke up. "No, my mom and dad had a big fight this morning."

"So did mine." Trevor was suddenly relieved he wasn't the only one with parents who fought.

"I'm sorry, boys. That's really hard, and I just want you to know that it's not your fault. Grown-up parents fighting isn't your responsibility. You aren't causing the fights. Even if they say they are fighting about you, it's not about you."

Johnny and Trevor looked at each other. It felt comforting to have their teacher understand and care, even though it didn't solve anything. Trevor liked that his teacher didn't try to fix it or him, she just cared.

Trevor quickly wiped a tear that slipped down his cheek. His teacher reached over and patted him on the shoulder.

"It's okay to be sad. Can you show me where you feel your sad feelings?" Johnny touched his belly and Trevor put his hand on his chest.

"That's good. Can you give your feelings a name?"

Trevor said, "I feel angry."

Johnny said, "I feel scared."

"Yes, you gave it a name. Way to go, guys. Is it your job to fix mommy and daddy, or is it your job to be able to name your feelings?"

"I think it's our job to name our feelings," both chimed in.

"That's right! If you can name your feelings, then you don't have to act them out. Okay, boys, go out and play, and if you need to talk, I am always here." With that, they dashed out the door—at least a little relieved.

TEN YEARS LATER

Trevor knew what it meant to feel lonely. He felt alone long before his dad slammed the back door and squealed the tires of his new sports car, tearing out of the driveway for the last time. After ten more years of bitter contention, Trevor felt a mixture of relief when his dad left for good; yet he longed for his dad in a strange sort of way. He always wished his dad was more like Jeff's dad: wrestling, roughhousing, giving him a pat on the butt when he did something great. His own dad could never engage with him like that; he treated Trevor like he was a stranger.

After his dad moved out, the only time Trevor saw much of him was at his baseball games. Trevor was a natural athlete and the one thing he knew how to do was to perform. He wanted to prove his worth so he pushed himself to excel at everything he did. In some ways, he wanted to be like his dad—top of the heap, smart, fast, and competitive. Yet sometimes those were the very things that repulsed him the most about his dad.

Keith hung around after the game to give Trevor a ride home.

"Hey, Trevor." Keith hid his unease behind his tense smile.

"Yeah, Dad—what's up?"

"Great game. You remind me of a younger me. I thought I would give you a ride home; I need to talk with you about something." Trevor shrugged his shoulders, as he followed his dad to the car.

"Um, well," his dad stuttered. "You know I have been dating Renee?"

"Yeah, I know all about it, Dad."

"Well, we are getting married next week, and I wondered if you wanted to be there?"

Trevor felt punched in the gut. It had only been three months since Keith slammed the back door and left him and his mom for good.

"Seriously, Dad! What's the hurry? You couldn't treat Mom decently. Do you think it's a good idea to get married so soon? You were the one who said you just weren't the marrying kind!" The long silence filled the air, as they walked to the car. Trevor noticed the new car smell, as he pulled his long legs into the compacted front seat. He wondered why Mom struggled financially while Dad bought a hot, new sports car every year.

"She's pregnant…"

"Who's pregnant?" Trevor demanded.

"Renee. Renee is pregnant."

"Seriously, all those years of tears when month after month Mom couldn't get pregnant and now, not only have you left her, but you are going to have a baby with the woman you cheated on Mom with? That hurts! How is Mom going to take that? She already cries herself to sleep. I can hear her when I walk past her room, you know—she's so sad. I can't imagine what this will do to her!"

Keith didn't say a word; Trevor turned his head and looked at him. His jaw was clenching and Trevor wondered how far he could push this conversation. His dad wasn't the type to have deep conversations, let alone the kind that made him look bad. His dad loved to win and usually fell apart if someone gave him a reality check.

"I don't know what to say to you, Trevor. Yeah, I have screwed up with you and your mom, but none of it is my fault. I tried. You don't know, but I tried. I can't help it if I couldn't give her a baby. I got you for her—isn't that enough?"

Another punch to the gut. His adoption comment stung. Trevor was reminded how he was supposed to be the child who filled his mother up and resolved the tension in his parents' marriage.

"So are you saying if I wasn't such a disappointment Mom wouldn't be so unhappy and you two would still be together? Seriously, Dad, can't you ever own anything?"

Trevor wanted to say more, but instead shut his mouth and thought about the words he wanted to spew at his father. Not once when his dad lost it had he ever apologized. Never had he heard his dad be tender with his mom. She was a sweet woman—sad, but sweet. Trevor felt the weight of his mom on his shoulders. He was already the main person who tried to help her cope with the divorce and now this?! Dad having a baby with the woman he left mom for—this should go over well. Trevor stewed in his cynicism. He climbed out of the car, slammed the door, and grabbed his gear from the trunk. He didn't look back to say goodbye.

THREE YEARS LATER

Trevor hung up the phone; his stomach was tight with tension. The conversation with his mom was typical. She was warm, kind, and caring, but after she asked Trevor about how he liked college, she went into the usual routine.

"Trevor, when can you come home? I'm so lonely and I really miss you. Besides, I need you here. Without your father, I miss having a man in the house!" The guilt she piled on and the way she clung to Trevor made him want to run and hide or escape in some way. He experienced a wave of heaviness crashing over his head. He felt as though he were drowning, as if there were no oxygen available, like there was no sliver of hope to escape this suffocation. He just listened until his mom was finished saying what she was going to say.

"Mom, I gotta go. I'll try to get home as soon as I can. I love you. Take care of yourself. Maybe you should consider dating a decent guy, not like the last several..."

Then he did what came naturally at this point in his life—more like a habit he couldn't shake. Whenever he felt overwhelmed or suffocated, he opened his computer and clicked on an all too familiar website. Pleasure and arousal filled him simultaneously with guilt and disgust. After finding a quick release, he wondered why looking at naked guys was where he found relief from the neediness of his mom and the longing he had for a real dad. The moment of pleasure was replaced with a feeling of disgust. *What if the other guys knew he looked at gay porn? Why couldn't he just be a normal guy and look at naked women?* he wondered.

Trevor had grown to hate himself. He always felt drawn to men who seemed like the real deal—like Jeff's dad. He wanted someone to wrestle with him, put him in a headlock, and teach him how to be a man. Instead, he watched men be sexual with each other. *What is that about?* he wondered.

He slammed down the lid of his computer and said aloud, "I've got to get out of here!" He fumbled his way down the stairs and was surprised to see Kevin, Jeff, and Jason hanging out on the back porch.

"You guys hungry?" Jason asked. Trevor wondered if Jason was always hungry.

"I could eat," Trevor responded, relieved to have a distraction and knowing he was hungry for something. The other two nodded, and they piled into Jason's jeep. On their way to Chipotle, Jason's phone rang.

"Hey, James, what's up? Yeah, great, we were just headed there—see you in about five minutes." Hanging up the phone, he said over his shoulder, "James is going to meet us for lunch."

They mostly wolfed down their food before the conversation went anywhere. Hunger muffled for the moment, James looked at the guys and asked, "So, how are you guys doing? How are your relationships?"

His question caught Trevor off guard. He was ready to bust so he spewed, "I'm drowning." The guys all looked at him.

James spoke first. "Tell us about it."

"My parents divorced three years ago. Don't get me wrong; I was glad. My dad was cheating on my mom and never treated her well. He called me lots of names and finally it got physical between us before he took off for good. He has another wife and two little kids now. I pretty much hate him. My mom is one of the nicest ladies you could ever meet. She loves me and I love her, but, man, every time I talk to her I want to explode!"

"What do you mean?" James asked.

"As long as I can remember, she has relied on me for support. I think it messes up my relationships with females. They sort of freak me out—if I get close to one, I feel smothered, and I'm terrified she will suck me dry."

"So, how are you dealing with all of this?" James wondered out loud.

Silence circled the table, as Trevor wondered how real he should be. James helped him out by saying, "Hey, I dealt with hating my dad by looking at a lot of porn. I didn't know that's why I was doing it. I just thought it was, well—fun. But then it took over my life, and it was all I wanted to do. So, there was this older man; he became like a mentor to me. He helped me see that my Family of Origin was pretty screwed up, and I was probably trying to medicate my pain with porn and sex. It made sense to me and he helped me walk through some healing. Now, he's helping me build a healthier relationship with Kaycie. I screwed that up pretty bad…"

Trevor identified with James. And Kevin nodded his head like he was connecting some dots as well.

"Yeah, porn is a pretty big deal in my life," Trevor admitted. Kevin just nodded again.

"I get it," James said. "I'm sorry. It's hard to be caught in the trap of porn. It's so conflicting—fun, relieving the stress for a moment, and then the guilt settles in."

The guys nodded their heads in agreement. Trevor felt comforted knowing he wasn't the only one.

"Hey, if you guys want to meet this man I told you about, my mentor, well, he leads some groups to help guys get freed up from porn and other stuff they are doing they don't want to do. Want me to see if he can do a group with you guys?"

"Sounds good to me," Trevor said.

"Yeah, me too," Kevin agreed.

Jason spoke next and said, "I want to come too; it's not like I have it all together in this department. How about you, Jeff?"

"Why not? Yeah—okay," Jeff agreed.

With stomachs full and hearts a little lighter, the guys finished up their drinks and headed home. It felt good to be honest with someone—someone safe, Trevor thought. Maybe there was hope for him yet.

WHERE TO GO FROM HERE

Shame and sexual addictions are agonizing for the person who is struggling. And like so many others, Trevor is searching for a male role model (someone or something to fill the void he is feeling) so he begins to medicate this void through same-sex porn. Which leaves Trevor feeling disempowered, sexually disoriented, and shamed.

All of us are meant to have a healthy attachment to our same-sex parent. We all need a role model—someone who can say "This is how you do life." This role modeling gives the child guidance. Yet, if this essential developmental element is missing from a child's upbringing, the child may experience sexual confusion later in life. This is not an *always* statement but a sometimes statement.

However, in some situations, as is the case for our character Trevor, the way the same-sex parent does life is repugnant to the child. Trevor is repulsed by his father's behavior. He knows he doesn't want to be the same type of male. He thinks, *I am a male, but I don't want to be like this male.* Trevor's father has not given Trevor any positive feelings about being a male. The result? Trevor feels sexually confused; he is confused about his sense of self, he is confused about his identity, and he is confused about his gender. Trevor's porn use is his way to medicate his shame and his pain; however, it only ends up bringing more shame.

Further, Trevor feels shame as it relates to his mother. His mother is needy and emotionally demanding, and Trevor knows he is unable to meet her needs. He internalizes his pain and feelings of inadequacy; and in turn, he feels even more emasculated—he thinks something is wrong with him and he is broken. He is enmeshed in the dysfunction of his family system.

So where does he go from here? Trevor needs to find some healthy male attachments that are not sexual. These relationships will provide containment (a safe place to be real and raw). These male friendships or attachments are like comrades he can do life with, and they aren't going to sexualize their relationship with him—they are going to be safe relationships. Trevor also needs a coach or mentor, like James in this chapter—someone who Trevor can identify with and learn from. Having healthy male relationships in his life will help him begin to heal and find freedom from shame and confusion.

Trevor needs containment. Containment? What is it? Containment is a word that means, "Let me vent, let me share my feelings without criticism." The idea behind containment is, "Nobody is going to try to fix me; nobody is going to get uncomfortable that I'm angry, or I'm sad, or I'm grieving, or disgusted, or I feel hatred. Nobody is going to freak out or get religious because I struggle with same-sex attraction." Containment means being or having a safe place to get all your emotions and feelings up and out without judgment or criticism.

Trevor has hatred toward his father right now, and instead of using Christian language like, "Oh, you just need to forgive your dad," or, "You shouldn't feel like that; it's not right!" he needs to be heard. Too often, people are uncomfortable with someone else's anger or pain so they start cheerleading them by saying things like, "Oh, it wasn't that bad," or they invalidate their experience by saying, "You just need to forgive your father."

To become a healthy human being, Trevor needs containment and validation (a safe person who's comfortable with his feelings). Someone who provides containment means they give a safe place for someone in pain to "verbally emote." Through containment, this person gives acceptance, which sounds like, "I'm so sorry that was painful for you. I accept that this was hard for you. I accept that you are angry. I accept that you are confused right now. I accept you."

Through containment this person also gives empathy, which sounds like, "I hurt with you. That was terrible. I'm sorry that happened." We validate others when we say, "I can see why you would feel this way." And by meeting these human emotional needs first, we validate their worth, their humanity, and their personhood.

Forgiveness is the goal at some point, but that doesn't come first. That will come after Trevor has been very real and raw. It is similar to when Jesus came into the temple and He saw how it had been perverted and turned into a market place. Jesus was raw and angry, and He let it out. And in the same way, sometimes we just need to allow others to let it out, instead of trying to fix them or patch them up—misusing Scriptures such as, "You need to honor your mother and father," or, "You need to forget the things that lie behind and move toward what lies ahead." Instead of these biblical ideas being a comfort, they feel more like a weapon used to shut people up. People need a safe place to vent, to get it up and out. If they receive grace, then eventually they will be able to receive truth.

When we start to understand that sexual issues in people's lives come from their history, it helps us have compassion. Maybe you could identify with Trevor in some small way. If so, here are a few thoughts for you to ponder before you move to the next chapter.

1. How has your Family of Origin affected your sexuality?
2. Who celebrated that God made you either a male or a female? Did anyone?

3. Who talked with you about healthy sexuality?
4. How did attachment go for you? What do you think those early years of your life were like?
5. Was your same-sex parent a healthy role model for you?

FIVE

Doing the Work of Healing

Healing is hard work. It's not for the faint of heart or the weak willed. It doesn't come easily and it usually isn't free. Healing requires sacrifice on your part and a determination to do whatever it takes to become a healthy human being. Scripture reminds us that where our treasure is, there is our heart. If your heart is to heal your life, you will need to invest in yourself. This will require investing money you may not feel you have. It will require time, time you may believe you do not have. It will require doing more than showing up. Too often, people bring their containers (bodies) to an event that could bring healing and then say it didn't work for them. Honestly, when the person is ready to heal, the healing process and the people you need to help you heal will appear. Are you ready?

GOING WHERE YOU
HAVEN'T GONE BEFORE

The unknown is frightening for all of us. Sticking with what feels normal is way more comfortable than facing the unknown. It requires you to go where you haven't gone before. But here is the promise. Jesus said He would never leave you or forsake you. He promised He would never send you out alone. He is for you and with you, and as David said in the Twenty-Third Psalm, "Even when I walk through the darkest valley, I will not be afraid, for you are close beside me." (Ps. 23:4; NLT).

This journey will include some moments where you feel like you are in the valley of the shadow of death. It will bring up memories you don't want to face. It will show you where your character structure didn't get developed. And it will cause you to grow in ways you never imagined.

I promise, if you go on this journey of growth, in the end it will be as Dickens wrote, "It was the best of times, it was the worst of times." As you walk through memories, it will feel very much like the worst of times, but, once you have done it, your life will take on new meaning and suddenly you will wake up one day and notice the sky is blue again, and the grass is green. You will find your joy. Deuteronomy 31:6 reads, "So be strong and courageous! Do not be afraid and do not panic before them. For the LORD your God will personally go ahead of you. He will neither fail you nor abandon you" (NLT). God will be with you every step you take, every memory you explore, and every tear you cry. He loves you.

You have survived the worst. Remember that. And now you are going to heal so you can move into the future God has for you without feeling like you have chains wrapped around your ankles holding you back. You may think this sounds selfish. I want to ask you a question: Is this selfishness or is it stewarding your life wisely? Research shows the best mothers are the ones who can tell their story. I would imagine that is true for fathers as well. Can you tell yours?

WHO NEEDS HEALING?

Some might be wondering, *Why do wives of sex addicts need to do their own healing work*? It is important to understand *addiction* is a family system problem. If there is an addiction in the home, it will affect every member of the family—whatever the addiction.

Addicts typically need someone to blame for their unmet needs, and, often, the wife gets blamed. She typically experiences a lack of emotional connection and sexual intimacy. She may have felt shame and humiliation because of his sexual activity. It can feel embarrassing to know others know your husband has cheated or prefers porn over having a real, sexual relationship with his wife.

There can be financial losses, and when the wife brings up a problem it somehow gets shifted back onto her. This is painful for the wife. I have worked with so many women who are in what I refer to as *trauma brain* after finding out about her husband's activities. The wife will need to break through her own denial structure.

I spoke with a wife of a sex addict the day before writing this and she said, "After twenty years I am done doing CPR on this marriage. All of these years I thought there was something wrong with me because my husband has never wanted me sexually. I held this carrot out, thinking if I lost twenty pounds, then he would want me. I didn't understand that his lack of desire for me had nothing to do with me. It had everything to do with his addiction. I love him, but I am done treating him like he is fragile, making excuses, covering for him, and taking all of the blame for our lack of emotional and sexual connection."

I was so proud of her; she was breaking through her denial and delusion structure. It takes a lot of courage to break through and most likely a woman will need support to do so. One side note, males aren't the only sex addicts. Females are suffering from the same disease. (If you are a male, married to a female addict, this applies to you as well.)

HEALTHY SELF

Not only do the spouses of addicts need support systems in place for their healing work to begin, but they also need to focus on becoming the healthiest possible version of themselves through self-differentiation. The truth is, we all grow up in some dysfunction, and all of us are raised by two imperfect people. If you are a parent, you know what I am talking about. However, in order for us to truly "be adults" we have to first see ourselves as part of the whole equation. But we can't stop there. Next, we must set our hearts on becoming all we can be—becoming our healthy selves—experiencing self-differentiation.

So what does self-differentiation look like and how do we start on this important journey? I believe the first step of becoming a healthy self is realizing we are loved unconditionally by God and He has a purpose for our lives. Once we know we are on solid ground and His love has been integrated into the soil of our lives, we can begin to develop a healthy sense of who we are. It is vital to grow a healthy self, in order to have a healthy marriage and healthy relationships.

Further, becoming a *healthy self* allows you to give back the shame to those who have tried to place the shame on your shoulders. God never intended for us to carry shame. Psalm 55:22–23 confirms this: "Pile your troubles on God's shoulders—he'll carry your load, he'll help you out. He'll never let good people topple into ruin. But you, God, will throw the others into a muddy bog, Cut the lifespan of assassins and traitors in half. And I trust in you." Clearly, God says we don't need to carry our troubles, our past traumas, or someone else's shame anymore.

For someone with trauma brain, it may be hard to know where to start, as it relates to your healing. And this is where story comes in. Again, I hope to show you more than tell you how the process and work of healing takes place. Kaycie knows she needs healing. She knows she suffers from trauma brain, and she also knows healing is a journey. So join me as we continue to discover her story.

MORE ROOM TO HEAL

Kaycie celebrated the progress she was making in therapy with Olivia, but she also knew there was more—particularly when it came to her sex life with James. Why was it so hard for her to share her body with him? Olivia was a sex therapist and she mentioned she led a group for women whose husbands have sexual addiction issues. Kaycie had resisted Olivia's invitation, but maybe it was time she went, especially after what happened the night before with James...

THE NIGHT BEFORE

James crawled into bed with Kaycie and reached to pull her body close to his. His hands gently caressed her. He wasn't doing it in a groping or demanding way. He was just rubbing her back and shoulder, but she could feel her body freeze. Message clearly sent, his warmth for her vanished, and he rolled over feeling rejected.

"James," Kaycie whispered into the darkness, "are you still awake?"

"Yeah," he eventually responded. After another moment of silence, he asked, "Why don't you ever want me?" His voice sounded broken.

"I don't know, James. I got so used to being angry with you about sex. How you hurt me—I put you in this ugly little box in my head, accusing you of being the typical male who only ever wanted sex. I decided you were just using my body for your pleasure and eventually came to the conclusion I held the keys to my body, and I didn't have to share it with you if I didn't want to. I know it sounds super selfish, but it's what I did, and now I can't seem to move past how I view you.

"I like holding the keys to the kingdom of sex and I don't want to let you back in. You hurt me once, well, more than once, and I'm not sure I can ever trust you again..." Her voice trailed off.

James let out a moan; he wanted to remind Kaycie of how far he had come from that selfish man who did just want to act out sexually on her body. He had been in treatment for his sexual issues for two years with his therapist and in a men's group as well. Did his progress not count for anything?

"I get it, Kaycie; I probably deserve it, but it really hurts. I try not to let it get to me, but sometimes I feel unwanted by you, and wonder if my body grosses you out or something, or if you will ever stop punishing me. I know I screwed up. I know I was selfish. I know I took from you. I don't want to do that ever again.

"I want to make love to you because I love you and when we truly make love there is something that happens deep inside my soul. I experience love for you that I don't have words for. It connects me in ways to you I can't express. I wish I were more like you and had words to tell you what you mean to me, but it seems like my body has a language, and when our two bodies come together and make love it's something mystical and almost spiritual. I don't take it for granted like I did when I was an immature jerk. I understand how valuable you are and that what we share is something to be protected."

"James, I compare myself to the women I know you looked at; I don't look like them and I never will. I have stretch marks from three babies, and my boobs don't look like they used to after nursing them for what seemed like forever. I rarely make it to the gym and something weird is happening to my thighs."

Kaycie let out an exasperated breath and continued, "Honestly, I don't know why you would want me. I don't feel sexy and I don't see what you see in me. I know I'm not fun in bed. If I was I would have been enough and you wouldn't have needed porn or that one-night stand." Her voice broke as she said the last part. Tears were running down her cheeks—there, she said it.

"Kaycie, I'm so sorry I hurt you by my actions and behaviors. I was an idiot. You are the real woman I want. The rest of that was fake and false and my way of escaping myself. It wasn't because of you. It was never because you aren't enough; it was because I had all of this pain inside. I wanted to just medicate it to make it all go away. The hurt from my family, my hatred of my dad, my insecurities, all of the relationships I screwed up— Kaycie, I was a mess."

"James, I want to let you in right now. I do. I appreciate how vulnerable and open you are being with me. It helps to melt the ice. But then, damn it—I hate this part—the minute I feel my heart wanting you, some stinging memory is right behind it. Especially how when I used to try to talk with you about this stuff you would just get defensive and blame me. That's the hardest part for me to recover from."

"Yeah, my defensiveness hurt us a lot. Defensiveness is what nearly destroyed us. I was told men have a warrior's relationship with emotions and any time you got emotional with me, I just got out my weapons and fired away at you and then you criticized me." He reached out and put his arm around her waist. "Babe, do you think we can find our way through this?"

The warmth of his body reminded Kaycie of how much she actually did love this man.

"I hope so, James; I want to." She allowed her body to fit into the curves of his and, like two spoons, they drifted off to sleep.

The next morning, with a decisiveness she hadn't felt in a long time, Kaycie hopped out of bed, grabbed her cell phone, and left her therapist, Olivia, a message.

"Hi, Olivia," she said into Olivia's message box, "I am ready. Sign me up for the group you have for women. I'm tired of feeling like a victim to James's past and I am ready to really dig in and do the hard work—whatever that is."

She disconnected the call, relieved. This felt hopeful and like she was empowering herself to move forward. She knew she couldn't do it alone and was tired of trying. Her pastor was always saying how we need each other (the body of Christ) to get healthy. He also said because we got hurt in our Family of Origin, the FOO—she always giggled inside when he said that— now we needed the FOG, the family of God, to become the healthiest possible versions of ourselves.

Shame kept her from moving forward. She realized now her shame had been paralyzing her. When she told James last night she compared herself to the porn stars and had body image issues, just telling him that somehow freed her up to pursue the healing she needed. Her trust had been broken. James betrayed her. She was lied to, manipulated, and years were stolen. Today she felt the courage to say *enough*. Whatever it took, even if it meant telling a group of women how bad things had become in her marriage—Kaycie no longer cared.

DESPISING THE SHAME

A day earlier, Kaycie found a moment without the boys and she opened her Bible to Hebrews 12:1. She recalled how it said Jesus despised shame. She pondered how Jesus was betrayed by His disciple, Judas Iscariot. He was stripped naked, beaten, spit on, had a crown of thorns dug into his scalp, was crucified on a cross (a death reserved for the lowest of society), and He decided to despise the shame. It gave her courage to think that if He could reject shame under those circumstances then so could she. She would despise all of the shame and get real with a group of women she probably didn't even know.

At this point of her healing journey, Kaycie trusted Olivia, but she wondered if she could trust other women. She had to admit she had a lot of jealous feelings toward women. When James was caught up in his addiction, she saw how he lingered a little too long when he saw a gorgeous woman. She also saw how he flirted with other women right in front of her, as if she wasn't in the room. Her blood still boiled at those memories. But with the memories came the determination she wasn't going to stay in this place any longer. Enough!

Olivia called her back and said, "Kaycie, I have one spot left, but here's the deal—the group starts today at one. Is there any way you can make it?"

"Let me see what I can do." Kaycie hit the end call icon and called James. "Come on, James, answer the phone," she said to no one. "James, glad you answered. I called Olivia this morning and left her a message saying I was ready to do her group. She just called me back and has one spot left. Here's the deal: the group starts today at one. I know this is crazy last minute, but this is really important to me—to us. Can you come home and take care of the kids for me?"

"Um, wow, I really want you to go. I have several meetings this afternoon. One of them is with a big supporter for the ministry, and I have been trying to get on his calendar for the last six months." After a moment of silence James replied, "No, wait— you wouldn't even need to go to this group if it weren't for my sexual addiction. This is more important; I will cancel and be home by 12:30."

"Thanks, James. That means a lot to me." Kaycie texted Olivia and said she would be there.

As Kaycie pulled into the parking lot at Olivia's office, she felt a wave of regret about making the phone call that morning.

What was I thinking? She admonished herself. *Whose business is it anyway that James and I have sexual issues. This feels way too scary—so shameful.* But then, Kaycie remembered Jesus who despised the shame and determined again, she would do the same.

With her heart beating and palms sweating, she made her way into Olivia's waiting room. Thankfully, she wasn't the first one there, and a friendly Texas girl stood up to greet her.

"Hi, I'm Mary Francis. I know with a name like that you would think you would meet me at a nunnery instead of a group for wives of sex addicts, but here I am." She smiled as big as a Texas sunset and threw her arms around Kaycie.

Kaycie's fears melted, at least in part, with the warmth of her new friend. Thankful, she realized maybe she wasn't some sort of frozen ice queen who drove her husband to seek pleasure elsewhere. Mary Francis had enough warmth to melt any man and yet here she was.

Mary Francis looked about the same age as Kaycie and she happily told her about her family of two little toddlers, three dogs, and a goldfish, and of course her husband, Todd, who was her high school sweetheart.

"Right now he doesn't feel much like a sweetheart to me. I'm so spitting mad at him that I want to kick him to the curb hard, but dang if I don't love that man."

Kaycie liked her even more and could totally relate to her.

The other women eventually came through the door, some visibly fearful and one looking like she wanted to run for her life. About the moment Kaycie thought she would dash out the door, Olivia invited them back into her office.

Olivia had the chairs arranged in a tight circle and Kaycie noticed that as the women sat they scooted the chairs out to create some space around themselves. Olivia welcomed them and laid out a few ground rules for the group.

"I'm so glad you have chosen to be a part of this group. We will be together for most of this year, meeting weekly. I know it's a big commitment, but healing takes time. It doesn't happen overnight and you can't heal alone. You need relationships around you to heal. I want this to be a safe place for you to get the pain out and let healing begin. So, it's vital that everything said here stays here. Confidentiality is of utmost importance and I would hate it if you heard through the grapevine of this small town something you shared in this group. I also want you to commit to being here. You are a part of this group and your presence matters. If you must miss more than three times, please say so now."

The women looked at each other, assessing one another's commitment level to the group and if they could trust the women in this room.

"I'll share a little bit of my story first and then we can go around the room and introduce ourselves," Olivia said, as she made eye contact with each member of the group before continuing.

"My story is perhaps a little different than yours; I became interested in the effects of sexual addiction when I was in graduate school. We were required to do a research paper and for some unknown reason I picked the topic of sexual addiction. It wasn't until I was reading the fourth book and the twentieth article on the topic that I realized my father was most likely a sex addict.

"I remember sitting at my desk when the realization hit me. My father had porn stashed under the couch in the family room, like we kids wouldn't notice it there, and I am pretty sure he had affairs on my mom. He stayed out late more nights than he came home, and he sexually abused me as well.

"Before you freak out, I'm not saying men who struggle with sexual addiction sexually abuse their daughters, but we do know, when untreated, addictions can escalate. I'm sure my father never thought he would stoop to the level he did, but he did. When you add alcohol to the mix, people lose inhibitions and do things they wouldn't do sober.

"By the time I realized my dad most likely was a sex addict, I had spent several years in therapy working through my own trauma. I was part of a sexual abuse recovery group, and I healed enough I could actually feel some compassion for my dad. Not making excuses for him, but compassion in that he came from a family with tremendous amounts of dysfunction, he had personal trauma, and addiction was part of the culture he grew up in.

"It was important for me as a therapist to do my own healing before I asked other people to do their healing work. It actually helped me a lot to learn that my dad was a sex addict. I stopped taking responsibility for much of what happened to me and gave it back to him emotionally. I gave him back the shame; I realized I wasn't to blame for his problems. It was freeing to learn about sexual addiction. Now, in the last twenty years, I have worked with numerous sex addicts.

"This is what I have learned. Most come from a background of emotional abuse, and many have experienced sexual and physical abuse. These men are broken and hurt and wounded and have learned how to medicate the pain with sex. Most are hurt boys living in men's bodies.

"But I have no illusions. Recovery from sexual addiction is grueling work and requires a willingness to get real. I also realized sexual addiction impacts the family system. My mother struggled with depression. She was often sad. My siblings have struggled with addictions. I had to work through my strong tendencies to want to please others, take care of others, help their lives be better. I was trained by my mother to be a good little codependent. I had to own that and work on becoming a healthier self through self-differentiation and creating connections with healthier people. I have done a lot of work on creating boundaries for myself— learning to say, 'No,' or, 'That doesn't work for me.'

"My life has been and continues to be a work in progress. I remain a fellow traveler on this journey. I have found God's beautiful grace and the love and acceptance of others on this glorious journey. I hope you will as well." Olivia paused and looked around at the group of ladies gathered there.

"Would one of you like to tell us a little bit about yourself and your story?"

Sitting quietly, the women looked at each other, hoping someone would volunteer to go first. And then—God bless Mary Francis. You have to love a girl like her. She just tells it like it is. Looking right at Olivia, she said with exasperation, "Well, last Saturday night, Todd wasn't home by ten like he said he would be. He was supposed to be working on his brother's truck, but when I called my sister-in-law she said he left about an hour earlier. Pissed, I called my mom and asked her to come over and stay with the kids while I went and found out where that man was. I had my suspicions, so I hightailed it down to his favorite bar. Sure enough, there he was at the bar with a beer in one hand and his other hand wrapped around the waist of some cute little blonde. I wanted to smash a beer bottle over his head. I nearly dragged him by his ear out of that place and threatened to call my attorney right then and there. What a dog! And this isn't the first time I have caught him messing around, and don't get me started on what I have found on his computer!

"I know it's not all him. I play some crazy games with that man. One minute I am lovin' him and the next I am screaming at him, telling him how much I hate him! He says I am a yo-yo, and he isn't sure which person he is going to get on any given day. Heck, on impulse, I went and got these implants, thinking bigger breasts would get his attention. The surgeon tried to talk me out of this size, saying they were too big for my small frame. I wouldn't listen, and now I feel like I am wearing a floatation device twenty-four seven!"

Frustrated, Mary Francis threw her hands up in the air and continued, "Why do I even want to stay with a man who cheats on me and looks at porn? Is there something wrong with me?"

Her blue eyes softened and filled with tears, as she asked the question hundreds of women have asked. "Am I the stupidest thing on the planet? Is our marriage real? Does he even love me?"

Betty, the woman sitting next to Mary Francis, with kind eyes and soft, wrinkled hands, reached over to Mary Francis and said, "Darling, you aren't stupid. You have invested your life in this man, and you have children with him—you aren't stupid."

Olivia asked Betty if she would like to share her story.

Betty looked at her hands she was wringing.

"My husband was caught fondling one of our grandchildren. It's not the first time something like this has happened. We have lost a relationship with two of our other children because their children said grandpa did the same to them. My husband had a really bad childhood. His mom died when he was young and his dad became ill and had to be hospitalized until he died when my husband was thirteen years old. From that time forward, he was on his own.

"I didn't grow up with much myself. My dad was a drunk and lost several businesses his well-to-do family gave him during the depression. Finally, they just gave up on him and he became the black sheep of the family. I grew up going to church, and I just thought if my husband and I went to church every week and prayed then everything would be okay. I still think it will be, but the judge who put my husband on probation said he had to participate in a court-mandated group—said I also had to attend a group, so here I am."

Stunned, the women didn't know what to say. Finally, Holly asked, "Betty, do you really believe going to church is going to be enough to heal your grandchildren and children from what has happened?"

Betty shrugged her shoulders and didn't answer. Another woman, Emily, had tears in her eyes, so Olivia asked if she would like to share with the group what she was experiencing. Her childlike eyes searched the women's faces in the group to see if she was safe to share her secret.

"I was sexually abused by my grandfather." A tear slid down her cheek, and then another and another. The two women on either side of her instinctively reached out to soothe her. Olivia encouraged them to ask before they touched her. She nodded her approval and one of the ladies put her hand on her shoulder and the other lady next to her gently held her hand. Her tears continued, as her petite body shook from the sobbing.

When her tears were mostly spent, Kaycie offered, "I'm so sorry, Emily. You didn't deserve to be treated like that. That was a horrible thing for your grandfather to do to you, and I hurt with you. Thank you for telling us. I can only speak for myself, but I want to be here for you so you aren't alone anymore." The other women nodded in agreement.

Olivia returned her focus to Betty and asked her how it felt to see the pain sexual abuse from a grandfather had caused Emily. "Does it help you understand your own grandchildren better?"

Betty nodded, "Yes, I can see how that hurt her. I haven't wanted to face the depth of how much harm my husband has done to our family. My denial hasn't helped, and I know I cover for him. I didn't want to come today, but maybe I need it, or I will probably eventually lose all five of my children and grand-children."

A bit uncomfortable with the somber mood, Mary Francis wanted to lighten things up, so she chimed in. "You aren't the only one who needs this group. Heck, I've had my head buried in the sand with my butt in the air, hoping all of this will go away. Once in a while, I come up for a breath of air and darned if the same problems aren't still there." With that comment, the women laughed and nodded their heads. Vanessa was the only one who didn't laugh. Instead, she watched the other women with a pained expression.

As the laughter subsided, Olivia sat back and watched the group begin to connect. A warmth filled her as she caught a glimpse of how these women would cry together and find grace, strength, support, and the courage to heal, in the year ahead. She was glad they had each other. She also internally acknowledged the work that lay ahead.

FINAL THOUGHTS

Olivia mentioned her father was a sex addict and how that impacted her life. For her own healing to take place, she had to first educate herself on the topic. It is hard to heal from something we do not understand. Olivia learned that sexual addiction typically begins (not always, sometimes a person becomes addicted because of exposure) at an early age, because people either experienced emotional neglect, physical abuse, or some sort of trauma. Combine these components and you have a formula for a lifelong struggle if healing isn't pursued.

Olivia's own father came from an abusive home; it was so combative he ran away when he was fifteen. He had head trauma from military service and riding bulls in the rodeo. He self-medicated with alcohol. He would swing from being rigid, excessive, depressed, and obsessive to chaotic, emotionally absent, angry, and defiant. His behavior was unpredictable, one moment he could be playful and fun, the next raging and very scary.

Perhaps you can identify with some of Olivia's father's behaviors. Once Olivia educated herself, she could stop taking responsibility for her father's confusing behaviors. Olivia could more clearly understand the dysfunctions she grew up believing were normal were anything but normal—but it wasn't her fault. She worked on becoming a healthier self (through self-differentiation), who had the right to be separate from her father and his issues, even though she was raised to believe it was her job to help take care of her dad. She began the process of giving him back his shame, acknowledging the damage done and growing herself up to become the woman she wanted to be.

Olivia focused much of her growth on grieving her losses and on doing the *separation piece* of work with her dad. She needed to self-differentiate. Self-differentiation is the ability to separate your emotional and intellectual functioning from other people. It is the ability to separate thinking from feeling. A self-differentiated person is able to make deliberate decisions as well as take personal responsibility for choices made, whether good or bad. People with low self-differentiation are more likely to become fused with the predominant emotions of significant others. Olivia could relate. Her dad had a powerful personality, and she became fused with him emotionally at a very early age.

Self-differentiation is also the internal ability to have a secure and solid sense of *self* in relation to significant others. It is the ability to preserve a degree of self in the face of pressure for togetherness. Differentiation of self is the process of finding balance, harmony, and interdependence in relationships.

In marriage, a healthily differentiated spouse can recognize personal feelings of anxiety, but they can calm and soothe their own angry and fearful feelings and ask for what they need, rather than being reactionary or blaming their spouse for unhappy emotions. He or she takes responsibility for personal values, beliefs, and thoughts, while negotiating conflict and closeness with his or her spouse. Destructive and reactive patterns are acknowledged and worked on by practicing new behaviors—creating new habits.

This self-knowledge does not rely on others for acceptance or validation because validation is centered on and found in Christ. When validation is centered in Christ rather than others, God is the source of acceptance and security. I'm not saying we don't ask other people to meet needs and provide us with acceptance, comfort, validation, and love. What I am saying is our part (our responsibility) is to partner with God to become a kind and loving parent to ourselves. To do this, we must practice letting His love in. The result? Our relationships will be based on love and desire, instead of need and desperation.

MOVING FORWARD

Here are a few thoughts for you to ponder before moving to the next chapter:

1. Have you taken the time to educate yourself about sexual addiction? Some call it the plague of the twenty-first century.

2. Are you taking responsibility for other people's issues? Who do you need to hand back a burden you have been carrying or trying to fix?

3. Do you find yourself trying to please others? Cover for them? Make excuses for them?

4. Have you committed fully to your own personal healing journey?

5. What holds you back?

SIX

Doing Life Together

G roup work is so fascinating because anything can happen. One person will share something which will trigger a thought or a memory in another person and so on. The reason I emphasize groups in this book is that, as I have mentioned earlier, we were meant to heal in the context of the family of God. Healing happens when people feel safe, and when someone feels safe, they open up and get vulnerable and truthful about their history.

In this chapter, the women will process some of their own traumas and begin the process of looking at their personal boundaries and attachment issues. Awareness is growing that, yes, their husbands have some sexual issues, but so do they. Let's face it; none of us have this topic completely figured out. Statistics show people are in one of three places when it comes to human sexuality:

1. They are in the process of working through a sexual issue of some sort.
2. They have just come through a difficult sexual situation.
3. They are about to discover a sexual situation that will require them to work through it.

I suppose we all have the choice to just get stuck and stay right where we are and hope the problem goes away. That is wishful thinking. We are called to partner with God in stewarding our lives, even our sexual lives.

OLIVIA'S PROCESS GROUPS

As the women settled into their familiar spot in the room, Olivia observed how the group was forming. She sensed they were connecting well, and safety and trust were being established. Olivia wanted to give the group more structure, so after checking in with everyone she started.

"Ladies, if you have just found out about a betrayal, I want you to remember you will most likely be in trauma brain for a period of time. It's important for you to know what's happening inside your brain, as well as your husband's brain. If you are experiencing brain fog, you are normal. If you can't remember where you put your keys, you are normal. If you are sad one moment and angry the next and then numb the next, you are normal. If you are wondering if your marriage is real and if the man you thought you knew is real, you are normal. He may be feeling much better because he has come clean. But you may feel miserable.

"Sexual addiction isn't about sex; it's about medicating some sort of pain or using sex as a way to cope with life. Wives of a sex addict, who just found out about a betrayal, can have the brain profile of a rape victim. This type of information, especially when it leaks out, meaning he discloses his story a little bit at a time, has the potential to traumatize your brain over and over again. This creates stress, which impacts the amygdala (integrative center for emotions, emotional behavior, and motivation), hippocampus (the part of the brain that is the center of emotion, memory, and the autonomic nervous system), and your prefrontal cortex (the part of your brain used for reasoning, memory, problem solving, and personality development).

"Trauma brain also increases cortisol and norepinephrine responses. For some people, if the stress is prolonged it can move into PTSD. We try to encourage people to get into a treatment program before they start telling their story so we can coach them on how to best tell their marriage partner about a betrayal. We also encourage the spouse to be in treatment so she or he has the support and care needed to help recover from the stress. Each of you will have different responses and that is completely normal. If this is the first major stressor in your life, your brain may handle it much better than someone who grew up with trauma. Please know this group is here to help you heal, and I know treating your brain is very possible. Getting the right amounts of support, empathy, grace, validation, feedback, and truth can help rewire your brain.

"Thankfully, God made our brains with *neuroplasticity*. In other words, our brains are continuously shapeable and moldable. With all this knowledge in mind, I think the most important thing we can do for ourselves and for our healing is to be aware of the voice of the critical judge—okay—so, some of you are looking at me thinking, *What is she talking about?!*" Looking around at each other, several of the ladies gave a soft laugh in agreement. Olivia smiled knowingly and continued.

"Okay. So let me explain what all this means. The *critical judge* is simply a voice inside all of us, typically shaming in nature. The voice will sound critical and judgmental and make us want to run and hide from others. Can any of you relate to that?"

Emily spoke up, "Yeah. I thought my grandfather sexually abused me because there was something wrong with me. He picked me because I was the quiet one and he probably thought I would never tell anyone. I have hated that I am more reserved by nature." The other women nodded sympathetically.

Olivia asked the group how they felt for Emily and what they thought of that critical judge.

Holly was the first to reply, "I can identify with you Emily. Now that I think about it, my critical judge has always told me my mom slapped me around because I wasn't very smart. I have dyslexia, and I have always felt less than…"

Kaycie chimed in, "My dad stayed out late at night and threatened to leave mom all the time. I begged him not to leave. I cried and screamed and promised I would be better if he just wouldn't leave me." Tears pooled in her eyes at the memory.

Olivia said, "Do you see how shame gets wired into our system at such a young age? Shame says you aren't enough. You are less than. You aren't a good enough wife, mother, friend, daughter. You aren't pretty enough, smart enough, and you don't wear the right clothes. The list is endless of how we aren't enough and then we hide because we believe what the critical judge is saying—we believe a lie. It's a hellish way to live life, but, sadly, it's how most people live. That is why we need a safe place like this group to challenge the lies of the critical judge. A safe place to receive feedback, validation, acceptance, support, and empathy.

"So let's talk for a minute about denial and what it really is." Olivia continued, "You may have had suspicions that something wasn't right in your relationship with your husband, but you felt too much shame to say anything, hiding in *denial*. Denial is part of any dysfunctional system. But our goal here is to care for your trauma brain and to make sure you experience grace and support in this group. When this happens, we will start to work on what the *truth* is." Olivia paused. "Okay. We are going to take a quick break here, so you can get up and stretch your legs. Also, please make sure to get some water. It's important to stay hydrated when you are dealing with difficult topics."

The ladies in the group nodded and then slowly, one by one, they stood up to either stretch or get water. The atmosphere seemed filled with expectancy and God's peace. For the first time, many of the ladies were beginning to see bits and glimmers of hope: hope that maybe their marriages and relationships would make it, hope that maybe there really wasn't something wrong with them. Maybe what they struggled with really was trauma brain, but their brain could be rewired. And with some work, their brains could be healed. Each woman was deep in thought as they slowly made their way back to their seats and settled in.

Olivia smiled. "So let's talk about what you can expect from me and our group during our times together. Over the course of this year, we will want to address any trauma from your past, such as how attachment went for you as a child, and any tendencies you may have to rescue, fix, control, or take care of others. We will work on you finding your voice and setting healthy boundaries. Drs. Henry Cloud and John Townsend wrote a classic book several decades ago called *Boundaries*. It is one of the best books on understanding and learning how to set boundaries in our lives. I love that they teach, 'Those with good boundaries have more love.' I've experienced that to be so true, and I hope you do as well, as you begin to form new and healthy boundaries.

"There will be grief work to do, so we will work on integrating the negative realities of life. For example, your husband may be a wonderful provider, care deeply for his children, love you and love God, and still have a porn addiction or have betrayed you in some way. This is possible because most people cut off the shameful parts of themselves and tuck them away in a hidden compartment.

"When we learn how to celebrate the good and grieve the negative, our lives become much more holistic. Negative realities are a fact of life in any and every relationship. Jesus promised we would suffer in this world and experience hard and even bad things. He said bad things happen to good people. You did not deserve the bad things that have happened to you—we live in a fallen and broken world, and evil impacts all of us. This is why we will do grief work, so we can become more integrated and whole."

"I love what God said in Isaiah 61. Let's take a minute and read this together. Isaiah 61:1–7 reads:

> The Spirit of God, the Master, is on me because God anointed me. He sent me to preach good news to the poor, heal the heartbroken, Announce freedom to all captives, pardon all prisoners. God sent me to announce the year of his grace—a celebration of God's destruction of our enemies—and to comfort all who mourn, To care for the needs of all who mourn in Zion, give them bouquets of roses instead of ashes, Messages of joy instead of news of doom, a praising heart instead of a languid spirit.
>
> Rename them "Oaks of Righteousness" planted by God to display his glory. They'll rebuild the old ruins, raise a new city out of the wreckage.
>
> They'll start over on the ruined cities, take the rubble left behind and make it new.
>
> You'll hire outsiders to herd your flocks and foreigners to work your fields, But you'll have the title "Priests of God," honored as ministers of our God. You'll feast on the bounty of nations, you'll bask in their glory.
>
> Because you got a double dose of trouble and more than your share of contempt. Your inheritance in the land will be doubled and your joy go on forever.

Again in Luke 4:18, Jesus says, "God's Spirit is on me...To set the burdened and battered free." He knew our hearts would get broken in this world, but He has made a way for those hearts to be healed. As you have already experienced, we will grieve the bad together, celebrate the good, work on healthy attachments, set boundaries, and continue to develop your adult voice.

"Does anyone have a 911 today? Anyone in crisis?"

Angie, an ER nurse started, "I think I hate him."

"Can you tell us more, Angie?"

"I knew on our honeymoon that I had made a mistake. But what could I do—I was stuck with him. I wanted kids more than I wanted a husband, so I had four kids with him. And now that I have the kids, I just want him and his need for sex to go away. I don't ever want him to touch me again, and he is always wanting to touch me. He needs to get out of my life for good!"

"You really want him to go away," Olivia responded.

"Yes, if he left, my life would be perfect," Angie said vehemently.

"You're convinced that if you could get rid of him, all would be well in your world," Olivia replied.

"Yep, I could do whatever I wanted, without him bothering me."

"Angie, is this about your attachment style or about him?" Olivia asked.

Angie popped back with, "It's about him of course; isn't that why we are here, because we are all married to a bunch of perverts?"

"I don't know, Angie. Is that why you are here?" Olivia responded. "Is your husband a pervert?"

"Well, he badgers me for sex," Angie grimaced.

"Does he demand sex from you frequently?" Olivia asked. "Or does he long to share sexual intimacy with you and maybe has an immature way of asking for that or initiating with you?"

Angie sat back in her chair and let out a deep huff. "I haven't ever thought of that before; I don't know if I care. I just want him to go away. I can take care of me and the kids—I don't need him anymore."

"Angie," Olivia probed, "Is this about what's going on inside of you or about your husband?"

Angie fired back, "I don't want a man in my life! They are too needy, and I feel suffocated by his presence in the house. I'm always running away from him. As a matter of fact, I run twenty miles a week, just trying to avoid him! I don't want to be close with him, and I sure as heck don't want to have sex with him. He makes me want to scream; I feel so mad and stuck!"

Kaycie inserted, "I feel that way sometimes with James. I fear being engulfed by him, and I don't know how to ask for what I need, so I just push him away. Sex is so close and intimate—I don't want to get that close either."

Holly asked, "So what happened to you two that you don't want sex or a man's skin on skin with you? I'm no professional, but I think something happened."

Everyone was all ears.

Angie spoke first, "Whatever it was I don't want to know, and I don't want to talk about it."

After a brief pause, Kaycie said, "I think I felt so powerless with my dad, I would do anything to make him stay to the point of begging him. It felt humiliating when he did finally leave, and I felt so alone, abandoned. I think I made myself a promise that I would never let a man hurt me like that again. And sex feels so vulnerable—I don't want to be that vulnerable with James. If I do, I will get too attached and then what happens if someday he does leave or cheats again? I can't take it. It feels too scary."

"How does it feel to say that, Kaycie? Have you ever given those emotions words before?" Olivia asked.

"No, never. And for the longest time, I've wondered if something is wrong with me, but now it makes sense. I haven't wanted to be hurt again, like my dad hurt me. Is this about my attachment style?" She asked to no one in particular.

"What do you think, Kaycie?" Olivia responded.

"I think it could be. I was always afraid of losing my dad, and so I think I became avoidant, to protect myself from getting hurt. James says I sometimes live in my own world and that I'm hard to reach. If he wants to be close, I can feel suffocated and want to run away. If we need to have a hard conversation, I make excuses for why I don't have time, or I just stay busy working on another project—even if it's just doing the laundry. I avoid getting close. It terrifies me. My dad leaving just proved the point; you can't trust men to stay."

Kaycie let a tear slide down her cheek. "Once in a while, especially when James and the boys are wrestling on the floor together, I notice an ache in my heart. Why couldn't dad have stayed and wrestled with me? Why couldn't he have stayed and told me I looked pretty, when I felt so awkward during those teen years? Why couldn't he have been there when I went on my first date? Why couldn't he have been there when I married James? Maybe I would have made some better decisions. I remember in junior high being so hungry for male attention I let the science teacher touch my breasts in the closet of his classroom. I felt so humiliated, but I wanted the attention. Is that sick?"

Olivia asked the group if two or three of them could give Kaycie some feedback. "What are you feeling for Kaycie? Do you think she is sick?"

Emily said, "Kaycie, I'm so sorry your dad wasn't there for you. I can only imagine how hard that was for you. I hurt with you and wish you would have had the love and acceptance you needed instead of feeling so abandoned and vulnerable for male attention. You aren't sick. You were hurt. It's okay. I accept you."

Now the tears really started flowing.

Olivia nodded at Holly, who wanted to speak. "Kaycie, you were a kid. It wasn't your fault your dad left. You weren't bad or inadequate; he left because of his stuff, not yours. You are enough. It's okay for you to let yourself be close to your husband. He sounds like an okay guy and like he has worked hard on building trust with you and taking care of his side of the fence. I don't want you to feel so alone. Thank you for letting us into your pain. I hope you feel supported and loved. You aren't sick; it makes total sense as to why you let the science teacher touch you. Besides, he was the adult and should have known better. Remember, you were a kid. I accept you and love you."

Mary Francis then added, "Kaycie, you have made some huge connections today. I'm super proud of you. I can relate to you in so many ways. You go, girl!"

Olivia sat back and asked if anyone else could relate to Kaycie.

Mary Francis said, "Heck, I can't remember the guys who I have let touch me. Some I let and some just took. I even made out with a girl in high school just to turn a guy on. I have had sex with guys at truck stops, in the back of pickups, and—well—you just name it. Talk about boundaries, I wouldn't know where to start." Suddenly Mary Francis looked like she wanted to throw up.

"What is it, Mary Francis? What memory are you having in this moment?" Olivia asked.

"Probably the memory that haunts me the most is how my mom washed me in the tub."

"What do you mean by 'washed me'?" Olivia asked.

"Well, she hurt me."

"How did she hurt you?" Olivia wondered.

"She would put her fingers inside of me," Mary Francis remembered, a look of anguish and disgust darkening her face.

Olivia asked, "Can you give what your mother did a name?"

"Yes—I guess you call it sexual abuse," Mary Francis said flatly.

"Oh, Mary Francis, I'm so sorry; she shouldn't have done that to you. That was wrong of her," Kaycie said.

Olivia asked, "What was that like for you, Mary Francis?"

"Well, it has made me wonder if there is something wrong with me. It has made me question my sexual identity: am I gay? I sometimes wonder if I fooled around so much with boys and men to prove to myself I wasn't gay."

"What made you think you were gay?" Olivia asked her.

"Well, it hurt when my mom did that to me, but it also felt good once I got over the initial shock. It felt warm and tingly and exciting. And she would talk to me in a nurturing voice. It was one of the few times she told me she loved me. She told me I was beautiful. I was so starved for her affection I sort of ended up enjoying her abuse. Is that sick or what?" Mary Francis stated flatly, grief framing her face.

Olivia said, "Remember when we talked about our automatic sexual response system? When our bodies are exposed to sexual stimuli they automatically respond. That's how our bodies are wired."

"Yes, I remember," Mary Francis said.

"Thinking about how we are all wired sexually, what do you think about your responses to your mother's abuse?"

"I think, maybe, I am more normal than I thought I was. I think I was a little girl who wanted her mother's time and attention and approval, and it's sad that sexual abuse was the way I received that. I think it has really affected how I think and feel about myself. It has impacted my sexual acting out and it's caused me to feel shameful. I've carried shame for so long and I'm tired. I'm so tired of feeling shame and hating myself. No wonder I didn't think anyone could or would love me unless I was putting out sexually. I was sexualized by my own mother, when I was far too young to be sexualized. I should have been able to be a child. I think I lost a portion of my childhood the day my mother touched me sexually."

"What do you wish for that little girl who still lives inside of you to know?" Olivia wondered aloud.

"I want her to know she is not dirty, she is not bad, she is not unlovable. She has value and worth and deserves to be treated with dignity," Mary Francis stated.

"Who needs to treat her with dignity?" Olivia asked.

"I do. If I don't treat her with dignity, no one else ever will," Mary Francis stated with conviction.

"How does it feel to recognize you will teach others how to treat you?" Olivia asked.

"It feels empowering. If I can't respect myself, no one else will. It starts with me," Mary Francis acknowledged, her eyes lightening with the realization.

Olivia asked, "Mary Francis, what do you need from the group right now?"

"I think I need acceptance," she said.

"In what way?" Olivia asked.

"I need to know if y'all still accept me—accept me in spite of what my mother did to me and how my body responded to her. Do I creep you out? Do you see me as less than? Do you think I am sexually so broken I can never be whole?" She pleadingly looked around the circle of women, her heart on her sleeve.

"I accept you, Mary Francis. I don't think you are broken beyond repair. I think what your mom did was broken. I imagine she had some severe woundedness of her own, and I wonder what happened to her. But I love you and I love your honest sharing with us today. I respect you for being so open and truthful. I think you are more dignified than ever to me," Emily commented.

Holly added, "I am so happy you've connected important dots today. You discovered what happened and how that impacted your life. I can see that little girl inside of you, and I think she is strong and resilient. I admire her for surviving so much and for telling us the truth today. I hope you keep allowing her to tell her story, give her a voice, and love her. She deserves to be loved. I love her. I love you. I know you are the same person, but it's like the little girl had to go into hiding and lost her voice. Today she got her voice back."

The women celebrated together. Only Vanessa remained withdrawn and silent.

Olivia smiled approvingly at the women gathered in the circle. "I'm so proud of you, Mary Francis, for letting us into your world and your story. That takes a lot of courage. And I'm proud of how you ladies are allowing her to open up without trying to fix her. This is what containment looks and feels like.

"Now, before we move on, I want to encourage you with something. As you are beginning to trust others by sharing your story, I want you to know God is working in your life and on your behalf. He gives His promise to us that He started a good work with us, and He won't quit until He is done. I want to read you a verse from Philippians 1:6. It says, 'There has never been the slightest doubt in my mind that the God who started this great work in you would keep at it and bring it to a flourishing finish on the very day Christ Jesus appears.'"

Olivia looked around at the women. "How does it feel to know God is on your side?"

One by one, the women responded by nodding and giving soft replies of relief. Vanessa was still rigidly sitting, engulfed in a cloud of discernible pain.

Olivia made eye contact with her and asked, "Vanessa, is there anything you would like to say or is there anything stirring inside of you that you would like to share with the group?"

"I told you, I don't want to talk about it! Besides, I am fine," Vanessa retorted.

Olivia knew all too well that "fine" was code for *there is so much inside of me, I don't know where to begin.* And that "fine" is a form of resistance, resistance to give language to reality.

"What was so hurtful, Vanessa, that you won't talk about it?" Olivia asked, following her resistance.

"I don't want to go there," Vanessa answered.

"You aren't ready to go there," Olivia replied.

"No," everyone could feel her heels digging in.

"Okay, let us know when you are ready. We are here to listen to whatever it is you won't talk about and to care for your heart when you are ready." Olivia knew to back off.

"What are boundaries?" Betty asked

"What makes you ask, Betty?" Olivia queried.

"I don't think I have any," Betty answered.

"Yeah, me neither," Holly interjected.

Olivia replied, "Dr. Townsend says it like this. Imagine you have a neighbor who never waters his lawn. Whenever you turn on your sprinkler system, your water only falls on his lawn. Your grass is turning brown and dying, but your neighbors grass looks great. If you would define the property lines a little better, if you would fix the sprinkler system so the water fell on your lawn, and if he didn't water his lawn, he would have to live with the dirt. He might not like that after a while. As it stands now, he is irresponsible and happy, and you are responsible and miserable. A boundary clarification would do the trick. You need some fences to keep his problems out of your yard and in his, where they belong."

Holly chimed in, "Well, isn't that a bit cold? You know, to just stop helping?"

"Has helping—helped?" Olivia asked.

"Not in my situation. I work so hard at making my husband happy and it doesn't help. He only gets worse, and his porn issues have gotten worse," Holly said.

"Mine too," Betty agreed.

"We can spend our energy watering other people's lives, while our lives are dying. We can spend our lives hoping the other person will change, and all the while, our souls are wasting away in misery. Or we can take ownership of what we let into and onto our property line and take full responsibility for the life God has given us to live. It's our choice. Whose yard are you watering?"

The group was quiet as they thought about it.

Holly said, "Probably lots of people, but especially my husband and kids. Isn't that what a good wife and mother does?" she asked.

Olivia asked, "Is there a difference between taking care of our husbands and children versus giving care?"

"What do you mean?" Holly asked.

"Well, when we don't have good boundaries, we tend to take care of others, which feels heavy, responsible, and liable. Life gets burdensome and we become controllers and even manipulators, trying to get people to do what we want them to do. It's a hard way to do life. When we give care, we can focus on loving others, offering ourselves to them, letting our yes be yes and our no be no. We can stay relaxed, knowing each person is responsible for themselves. We are responsible to bring our best self to others, but we are not responsible for them, unless the person is a small, helpless child, and then of course we have responsibility for that little person, until they can take ownership of their own lives."

Olivia continued, "However, your skin is your biggest boundary and if you had your skin violated, like I did as a child, then most likely you didn't develop your 'No.' As an adult, I found myself exhausted and resentful. I said yes to everyone, because I didn't want anyone mad at me. It was an awful and powerless way to live. It took work to grieve the fact that my skin was violated by my own father. And it took work to learn how to say 'No.' I had to have a lot of support from other boundary lovers, to learn how to say 'No.' And honestly, I had to fight for it, because the people around me... well I had trained them to take me for granted and to take advantage of me. Once I owned that and started taking responsibility for me and not for others, I felt empowered and less tired."

The women in the group seemed to be hanging on every word Olivia said. She took a short pause and then continued, "Dr. Townsend always talks about Proverbs 4:23, and how we are to guard our own hearts, for everything you do flows from it. I remember the first time I heard him say that decades ago, I thought, 'What? I am supposed to guard my own heart?' I falsely believed other people would guard my heart for me or at least God would. God wants to empower us to guard our own hearts. If we do, it will save our souls. If we don't, other people will walk right over it. Proverbs also says a doormat will soon be forgotten. I had to wake up to the fact that if I wanted to become a healthy adult, I would have to own my own property—my body, my soul, and my spirit. What do you think ladies, are boundaries an issue for you?"

The women looked around the circle and, with their own non-verbal expression, began acknowledging that indeed boundary issues could have a part to play in their life circumstances.

After checking her watch, Olivia looked around the group of women gathered. "Ladies, our time is up for today. Would you like me to start next week with teaching on boundaries?

The nodding heads affirmed Olivia's question.

"Do chapter eight in your workbook for next week. Would someone like to close us in prayer?"

Holly wanted to: "Father, thank You for this time together and for helping us sort through our lives and the bad stuff inside. Help us with boundaries and teach us how to guard our hearts. Amen."

With that the women headed out the door with goodbye hugs and promises to stay in touch.

FINAL THOUGHTS

Whenever we find ourselves in unhealthy relationships, we always have to take a hard look at ourselves. What about this person draws me in? What am I trying to redo? Does this person remind me of my dad? My mom? A sister, brother? Am I trying to fix something from the past? Am I acting out something done to me, but I have never given it words and used my voice to tell my story? Am I hoping what was broken in my childhood, I will fix in my adulthood?

What did you learn about yourself from these women's stories? Can you see how abuse, abandonment, or neglect in childhood oftentimes leads to sexual acting out, typically starting in the teen years? Can you see how Family of Origin dysfunction plays a big role in married life?

Vanessa is feeling resistant to really joining the healing process. Resistance is all around us and most of us have to take a hard look at how we are resisting the very things that could actually help us heal. It's not Olivia's job to heal the women in the group; she simply invites them and it is their decision if they are going to join in or not.

God is inviting you into a healing process as well. Take a few minutes and write your answers to the following questions.

1. Which woman do you relate to and why?

2. Have you avoided closeness? Or do you feel anxious if there has been a disruption in closeness?
3. What makes getting close to others frightening?
4. Are you like Angie, in that you believe if you could get rid of a person in your life all would be well? Or perhaps, if you could get rid of your husband, all would be well? Try to explain your thinking.

SEVEN

The Guys' Group

James asked Ted if he would be willing to lead a group of young men, that he was mentoring, into sexual wholeness. Since Ted was retired, he had pretty much made mentoring his mission in life. Ted led several groups and happily agreed to add one more to his "retirement life," jokingly adding he was busier in retirement than when he ran a large counseling clinic.

Ted had been James's therapist and group leader for the last three years and because of the work he did with Ted, he felt like a new man. Ted knew when to push and when to give love. Ted struck that needed balance of being relational and warm, but not willing to put up with the lies and excuses. James experienced both. He knew Ted loved him like a son and yet wasn't hesitant to get into James's face if he was lying or minimizing the impact of his sexual behaviors.

Ted encouraged him to face and deal with his Family of Origin (FOO) issues, which James admitted he totally wanted to minimize and deny. But Ted wouldn't have it and pushed until James got real. And it was Ted who held him like a toddler when he finally grieved the abuse and neglect. Ted was the medicine and mentor James needed to break the stronghold of sexual addiction.

Now James wanted these four young men he had grown close with to experience the same thing—freedom. He didn't want them to nearly destroy their marriages and futures the way he had. As James reflected on what recovery meant to him, gratitude filled his thoughts. In retrospect, he wouldn't change a thing. The trauma from childhood, the hell he and Kaycie went through—it all had led them to recovery. And recovery felt good. He and Kaycie did the hard work and now they could see different fruit growing on the tree of their lives.

James introduced the guys to Ted, humbly admitting, "This is the gentleman I told you all about. He is the one who saved my marriage. I owe this man my life, and I'm so grateful he took me under his wing. He is the first older man I have ever had a trusting relationship with. He always told me if I couldn't relate to other men in a healthy way, I would never learn how to have a healthy relationship with Kaycie, where I wasn't sexualizing her."

Turning toward Ted, James continued, "If I haven't told you lately, thanks, Ted, for all you have done for me." James's voice caught with the emotion he felt for this man. Ted stood up and put his arms around James, saying, "I love you son."

Kevin peered over at Trevor to see what he thought about all of this man love. He had never seen anything like it and it made him feel a little uncomfortable.

James picked up on it. As he sat back down he said, "It's okay guys; he's like a dad to me and I think he will become that for you as well. A lot of guys who struggle with porn and/or unhealthy sexual behavior never had a dad who engaged with them.

"Ted, do you want to start with your story? I have already gone over the ground rules with the guys and they know my story."

Ted looked at James and nodded, and then he looked around the room at the four young men around him. How many groups like this had he led over the last four decades of his life, he wondered. A warmth filled his heart as he thought about how many men he watched find redemption for what was broken in their lives.

"Hi, I'm Ted. It's good to be here with you." Ted didn't waste any time getting to it. "I never knew my dad and the four men my mom chose to marry weren't good men. You could say her "man-picker" was broken. She worked at a bar to keep a roof over our heads and food on the table. It was just the two of us, unless she was giving marriage a try. But none of those lasted for long. She drank too much and she tended to pick men who did as well. Alcohol can be like gasoline on a fired-up relationship. Several of these guys busted her up pretty good. When I got old enough, I tried to defend her and that... well that never went well. There was always something about old man muscle that out-powered a teenage boy.

"By the time I joined the military at eighteen, I was angry and filled with hatred for authority. I had a burning need to outrun the anxiety and depression that haunted me—the memories, the trauma. I stayed high on my adrenaline and fueled it with my anger and aggression. I was always ticked off and messed up every relationship I had with a woman. I overreacted to everything and pushed everybody away who tried to get close to me. I was defensive and needed to be right; if anybody intimidated me, I gave it back tenfold. I was a real success at boot camp. I did my fair share of running extra miles, getting my rear end chewed out by the sergeant, and, basically, having a horrible time. Until I decided I wanted to win and get even and be at the top of the heap.

"Somewhere along the line, I had the idea I was going to be a pilot and be the best fighter pilot the military ever saw. I would prove everyone wrong. Yeah, my dreams came true, but I was miserable. Until I met a girl. She has been my wife for nearly forty-five years. If it wasn't for her, I would probably be dead. She loved me for some crazy reason. I wasn't good to her. But she is the one who showed me the love of God and led me to the Lord. An older woman mentored her and it was this woman who helped me grow up and get sober from the alcohol I abused and the porn I was hooked on. I went on to get my Ph.D. in psychology and have spent my life helping other guys like me find redemption.

"Buckle your seat belts gentlemen. I have seen hundreds of men healed from this drug called porn, but I have also seen plenty of guys who thought they could whip this dragon by themselves crash and burn up everything that mattered to them.

"Here's what we are going to do, gentlemen. We are going to tell our stories. The reason we do this is that your story will uncover what happened to you and why you do what you do. You didn't just fall off of a turnip truck and end up hooked on porn and acting out in ways that aren't good for you. Your history has impacted you, just like mine did me. Most men want to deny it and believe if they just ignore it all, it will just go away. Everything is fine. Baloney. It doesn't work that way. And so we are going to look at your story from every side, because if you have a pebble in your shoe and you don't remove it, eventually it tears a hole in your foot and lodges itself in your flesh—then it gets infected and inflamed.

"Eventually, if you don't have that pebble removed, you will end up with either a serious limp or have your leg cut off. You will say to me, 'Ted, why are you asking me about that again?' Here's why: it's like a football game—you know how they film every play and if something happens they replay that film from every possible angle to come to the truth. That's what we need to do with your lives gentlemen, if you are going to heal and have healthy relationships. It will be some of the hardest work you have ever done, but I promise it will be the best thing you have ever done. And if you do the work, you will get healthy. Much of the work we will do is grief work. Yep, you are going to learn how to grieve the bad stuff that has happened to you. But if you don't, you will keep medicating the pain with something: work, women, porn, sex, alcohol, food, success—you name it—we all do until we get that pebble out of our soul. Maybe yours is a pebble, some of you have some boulders, whatever the size doesn't matter, what matters is you are all in. What do you say, gentlemen? Are you in?" Ted looked each man square in the eyes.

A little afraid, a little unsure what to think, Jason said, "Yes, sir." The other three wide-eyed young men nodded their heads in agreement with Jason.

"You men are young. You may not have hit bottom yet or tried hard enough. I hope you're ready, because I would rather you do this work now than when you are fifty and have blown through a couple marriages or ruined your life in some other way. Here's what I do know; you can't heal alone. Jesus didn't do life alone. He chose twelve men to do life with and, heck, he is a member of the Holy Trinity. I imagine if he didn't do his earthly life alone, then maybe we shouldn't either. So who wants to tell their story?"

"I have something to say," Jason volunteered as he turned to Kevin. "I owe you an apology. I told you Grace and I almost went all the way, but I stopped before we did. I was too embarrassed to tell you the truth. The truth is—Grace is pregnant." Jason put his head in his hands and let the emotion out along with the secret he had been keeping from his newfound friends.

"People think I'm some sort of hero because I'm the captain of the football team, because I'm a Christian, and I try to walk out what my parents taught me. But man, I blew it with Grace. She called me last week and said she is pregnant. I feel like such a jerk. How could I have done this to her? She is the sweetest girl in the world and I was taught it is my responsibility to protect her. I haven't told my family. They are going to be so disappointed in me. I am their oldest kid. I have always tried to do the right thing, and now I haven't."

James turned to Jason and asked, "Hey, buddy, I hurt with you, and I can only imagine how surprised you are. I get it. But I have to ask you. Did you force yourself on her or was it mutual?"

"No, man, I would never do that. It was totally mutual. We both wanted each other. I just feel terrible, because I let her and everyone else down. I guess I have prided myself in being a perfect Christian. And truth is, I'm not. I think my pride has tripped me up, and I believed I was above doing something like this."

"Jason, what are you feeling?" Ted asked.

"I feel ashamed of myself."

"Kevin, how do you feel about Jason?" Ted asked.

Kevin turned to look at Jason, "I still think you are one of the best human beings I have ever met. You have been a true friend to me when I really needed a friend. Heck, I know you don't have the issues I do, but you showed up here today to support us and you are the first one, besides Ted, to get real."

Jason said, "Thanks, Kevin."

Ted loved these young guys already. "Jason, what's your biggest fear?"

"Well, I have heard my pastor back home say, on more than one occasion, 'If you have premarital sex you are messing up your chance to have a faithful marriage.' He said something like, 'If you have premarital sex'—I think he called it sneaking-around sex—'you will never have fulfilling sex in your marriage. Once you taste sex fueled with the passion of doing something you shouldn't be doing, married sex will be boring and you will most likely cheat on your spouse later in life.' I have also heard that if you get pregnant before you get married, you are going to curse your kid or something. I'm terrified that I have messed everything up! I'm terrified that the marriage Grace and I have been dreaming of will never be the reality we hoped for and my mistake will be a curse to this poor kid we have created together. I can't really think about anything else."

"Jason," James said, "I think what the pastor may have been trying to say is when sex gets paired with adrenaline it can be a rush some people get hooked on. And when sex is about getting a rush, married sex can be boring because this couple has used sex to get a high instead of sex being an expression of love. A couple like that then needs help in redefining married sex, just like Kaycie and I have needed help.

"Remember, most of us need to be *rewired* sexually. But it's never hopeless and you definitely aren't cursed to live in the dungeon of sexual doom. Here's the thing we have to remember: God is the God who redeems, not some of our mistakes, but all of them. Have you asked Grace to forgive you?"

"Yeah, we spent hours on the phone last week. We talked it all through and I asked her to forgive me. She said, 'Jason, let's be honest. We have waited for five years; I wanted you as bad as you wanted me. I forgive you. Will you forgive me?' I told you she is the sweetest girl alive. I can't wait to marry her and spend the rest of my life loving her and creating a family with her."

"Then, Jason," Ted said, "Don't let anybody put you under a bucket of shame. I believe you and Grace will have a joyful and fulfilling sex life together. David and Bathsheba didn't get off to a great start. As a matter of fact, their first sexual encounter had nothing to do with love and everything to do with David's lust and using his power in an abusive way; and yet they eventually become parents to one of the greatest monarchs in history. Don't let anyone speak words over you and Grace that will steal from you or this child. Our past mistakes do not define our future promises."

"I think I need to know you all don't see me as the biggest hypocrite in the world," Jason finally said.

"Guys, can you respond to Jason? Do you think he is a hypocrite?" Ted asked.

Trevor spoke up, "No, I don't, and, like Kevin said, you have been a real friend to me too. I know you love Grace and how committed to her you are. It's okay, man; we all screw up."

"What's your next move?" Ted asked.

"I am going to marry that girl, as fast as I can." Jason smiled.

"So here's the thing. Everyone messes up sexually, whether it's too much of something or too little; rarely do we humans get this thing right. We all need God's redeeming touch on this area of our lives. And for most, there are deeper issues at play here."

Ted asked the guys, "Can anybody relate to Jason—the shame he feels?"

"Yeah, I can," Kevin said. "I have lots of shame. I think the porn use has affected me in some freaky ways. The last time I was with Kate, my old girlfriend, I couldn't even get it up. I Googled it and read that watching porn and taking care of yourself can eventually lead to erection issues. I was so humiliated; I haven't even called her since I came to Texas. How's that for letting someone down—literally?"

Kevin, do you know what drove you into porn?" Ted asked.

"I think I do. My mom died when I was young; she was the most important person to me in the world. I loved her and could count on her. But she and my dad divorced when I was just a little guy and I didn't care that much for my stepdad. So when Mom died, I had to go live with my real dad, who I hardly knew. He drank a lot and slept around, and I pretty much raised myself. I think it was my loneliness that made porn so appealing. Beautiful women looking like they wanted me made me feel less lonely, at least for a few minutes," Kevin said flatly.

Ted said, "That sounds lonely, son."

"Yeah, it was super lonely. Since my mom died, I have felt very alone."

Ted stood and grabbed an empty chair, which he set in front of Kevin.

"Hey buddy, let's put your mom in this empty chair. I would like you to tell her how it felt for you when she died."

Kevin looked at Ted like he had to be kidding. "Really, you want me to talk to an empty chair and pretend my mom is sitting in it?"

"Yep. I know it sounds weird. You will just have to trust me, son. Just talk to her like she is sitting there. Can you picture her?"

"I guess so," Kevin resisted.

"Tell us what she looks like, son," Ted nudged.

After several moments of silence, Kevin finally said, "She is pretty. She is smiling at me, and I can see the love she has for me in her eyes. She has a kind face. I look a little like her."

"That's good. How about if you ask two of the guys to come and stand behind you for support?" Ted encouraged.

"Um, Jason and James," Kevin picked.

They stood up and got behind him with their hands on his shoulders.

"Mom," Kevin started, "when you died, I remember crying myself to sleep at night. I felt all alone. Why did you leave me? I was so angry; I hated God for taking your life. I hated my stepdad for not wanting to keep me. I was so alone and I was too young to have to experience that. I miss you every day of my life. I have felt so empty without you." Kevin's tough demeanor shattered as he let the grief flow out of him. He cried—hard.

The men in the room waited and felt the pain and loss with him. Time lapsed, as Kevin wiped his tears on his shirtsleeve. James handed him a wad of tissue. Jason and James squeezed his shoulders and gave him man hugs.

"Proud of you man for letting that out," James assured him.

"This is how it works, gentlemen. We have to get the pain out, face it, and grieve it, so we can stop medicating it. Well done, Kevin. How was that for you?" Ted inquired.

"Weird, but good. I had no idea I had all of those feelings inside me. I haven't felt those since Mom died," Kevin said.

"What do you need from the group?" Ted asked.

"Heck, I don't know—am I supposed to need something?" Kevin asked.

"Right, most of us don't have a clue what we feel or what we need. But to become a healed and whole man, we have to tap into what we are feeling and what we need. So just take a stab at it, Kevin. Do you need acceptance? Validation? Comfort?" Ted asked.

"Well, I actually felt comfort from James and Jason. Trevor, do you accept me? Or do you think I am some weird guy from LA?"

Trevor responded, "Actually, I think I need to do what you just did before I explode. I totally accept you. I wish I could do the same thing."

"Trevor, tell us how you might explode?" Ted explored.

"I told the guys how I hate my dad and how needy my mom is—I have a porn problem," He confessed.

"What kind of porn problem?" Ted asked.

Trevor's brain registered fear, as he wondered how real he should get.

"Man, Ted, I don't know if I am ready to say."

"It's okay, son, we are here when you are ready. Would you like to get it off your chest?" Ted asked.

Trevor hung his head and couldn't make eye contact with the rest of the group.

Ted continued, "Hey, Trevor, look at me, son. I accept you no matter what. There is nothing you have done that will change how I feel for you."

"I'm afraid the rest of the guys will not want to hang out with me if they know the truth," Trevor confessed.

"You are afraid. Can anyone relate?" Ted asked.

"I was terrified to tell you all about me getting Grace pregnant," Jason admitted.

"I have stuff even you don't know about, Trevor," Jeff confessed.

"Okay—this is hard, but, for some reason I can't figure out, I have been looking at gay porn," Trevor said, as he looked at his feet.

"You have been looking at same-sex porn," Ted replied matter of factly.

"Yes, and I'm super confused. I like girls. I mean I think they are pretty, and I feel attracted to them, but gay porn does something for me," Trevor said.

"What might it be doing for you?" Ted asked.

"I don't know if it's just about the turn-on or if there is something more—some need?" Trevor replied.

"What do you think that need is, Trevor?" Ted asked.

"I'm not sure," Trevor answered honestly.

"That's okay, son. You don't have to figure it all out. We will just create a dialogue in this group. Sexual thoughts, feelings, or fantasies are all okay to talk about right now. You can ask any questions you have about sex. I'm happy to listen to you, as you think this through. I think the most important thing isn't necessarily figuring out why you look at gay porn, but more importantly, what are your values, how are your relationships, and what choices are you making. I want to support you, as best I can," Ted reassured.

"Thanks, Ted. I haven't ever had anyone to talk with about this stuff. I have been trying to figure it out on my own, and honestly, it's all pretty confusing."

"Yeah, I get that, son. So, besides the porn, what else is going on with you?"

"I have felt responsible for my mom, as long as I can remember."

"That's heavy," Ted responded.

"Yeah, it is. Suffocating at times. I feel like I'm supposed to be her replacement husband."

"Trevor, you can't be your mom's surrogate spouse. That's not your job. You are her kid, not her husband. How would it be for you to start setting some limits with mom and thinking about becoming your own man—separate from your mom? I don't mean you don't love her and respect her. I just mean you work on making your own choices and taking full responsibility for your life and allowing her to take full responsibility for her life."

"That would feel good. Do you think I am—too close with my mom?"

"I don't know, son. What do you think? Are you enmeshed or codependent with your mom?" Ted asked.

"What does enmeshed mean?" Jeff asked.

"Typically, people in enmeshed relationships have difficulty knowing they are actually in an unhealthy relationship. An enmeshed relationship between a mother and son may look like this: Mom is all about mom, while the son is the person who lives to give to his mom. Mom knows her son is the only one she can depend on to help her and listen to her. The son is afraid to stand up to his mom, so she exploits his willingness to give to her. It's draining for the codependent and admitting it is an unhealthy relationship is the first step in making positive changes."

Trevor looked around the room, and asked Jeff, "What do you think, Jeff? You have known me forever. Am I enmeshed with my mom?"

Jeff sort of laughed. "Dude, you have been taking care of your mom since you were six. She is a sweet lady, but seriously, it's like she is emotionally twelve."

Trevor rubbed the stubble on his youthful chin and said, "You are right; I have been. It's exhausting. How do I stop? It's been my job for so long that I don't know how to do life any other way."

James jumped in, "It feels really normal for you to take care of your mom. How has that kept you from owning your life?"

Trevor pondered that. "Well, I stay focused on her problems, instead of my own issues or planning for my future. I think about her constantly and worry about her; I feel anxious and afraid she will make another bad decision. So I try to control her and tell her what to do, which she doesn't like. It's exhausting, and when

I get super frustrated, I turn to porn. I think same-sex porn makes me feel powerful."

"You have felt powerless to fix your mother and gay porn makes you feel powerful and in control. I get that. I had to set boundaries with my mom," Ted said. "She was a single mom, just like your mom. I had to learn how to say, 'Mom, I love you, but I can't figure that out for you. You will have to do that. Someday, if you really can't take care of yourself, I will be here for you, but, Mom, you are capable and it's not my responsibility to take care of you. I care for you, but I can't take care of you. I love you, and I am for you, but it won't work for me to do what you are asking from me.'

"After this conversation, I started to own my life. It started when I set limits with her. And I actually started to feel sort of like a man. It felt good to love her, but not to enable her." Ted asked, "What do you need from us to start setting limits with your mom?"

"It helps to hear you had to set limits with your mom, Ted; thanks for sharing that with me. It gives me permission to learn how to do the same," Trevor replied.

"Just practice something new, son. Learn to say, 'No, that won't work for me.' Do it with kindness and love, but give yourself permission not to take care of her anymore. This is a big deal for you, in becoming a healthy male." Ted looked around the group. "Jeff, you have been quiet. What's going on inside you?"

"I'm just taking it all in. I'm good; everything is fine with me." The stiffness in his delivery was not lost on the group.

"Hmm," James thought aloud. "You don't sound convincing. What's really going on?"

"I'm just thinking about something that happened to me and Trevor," Jeff said, looking at Trevor. "Not sure I want to talk about it though. And I'm not sure if Trevor wants to talk about it—we never have."

"This is the time and place we talk about the stuff we don't want to talk about," James assured him.

"Trevor, do you know what I am thinking about—you know, your neighbor?"

"Yeah, I know." His face turned blotchy red. "Go ahead and tell them. We are going to have to tell them sometime. We might as well do it today," Trevor said, still gazing at his shoes.

"So, Trevor and I have been best friends since first grade. We lived in the same neighborhood, played with the same kids, and got in trouble together. Well, there was this older kid who lived next door to Trevor. He would ask us if we wanted to come over and see the go-kart he was building in his garage. Then he asked us if we wanted something to eat, so we went inside. Nobody was home and he had some sort of movie playing. We got food and sat down to watch it, when all of a sudden the show got nasty—dirty—a woman doing stuff to a man and him doing the same thing to her and then another guy doing the same thing to the other guy.

"I had never seen anything like it before. I was scared and fascinated at the same time. I looked at Trevor and said we'd better go, but he seemed—you seemed frozen. It wasn't long before the movie was over and this neighbor suggested we let him do to us what we just saw on the TV—so we did.

"We went back several more times, until my mom found out and she said he was way too old for us to go into his house. We were only ten and he was sixteen. So we never went back and we have never talked about it," Jeff confessed.

"Man, I'm sorry, you guys. That was wrong of the older neighbor to expose you to adult sexuality. You were kids. You didn't deserve that to happen to you and it wasn't your fault. You deserved to be protected and not to have an older teenager, who knew better, perform oral sex on you. Was there anything else he did?" Ted explored.

Trevor said, "He eventually asked us to perform oral sex on him. Jeff never did, but I did a few times."

"Trevor, I hurt with you, buddy. That is super confusing. Was that your first sexual experience?" Ted asked.

"Yeah, it's like it got seared in my mind, and I can't forget it. It was my first sexual release. Now, I feel stuck there and can't seem to move forward," Trevor admitted.

"For sure, sex often gets stuck wherever it got started. What is fired together gets wired together. Your brain registered that as a powerful sexual experience, and that is still the sexual stimulus that turns you on. God wired all of us to have a sexual response system and if we are exposed to sexual stimuli, it is arousing. It's pure and simple biology. God wanted us to be protected from what we get exposed to. He never wanted you two boys to be exposed to sex in a way that felt shameful and dirty. God wanted you to learn about sex in a healthy way— ideally from a mom and dad who can talk about sex in an informative, age-appropriate way.

"Unfortunately, we live in a fallen, broken, sexually con- fused, messed-up world. God didn't want any of you guys to get exposed to porn, adult sexuality, or unhealthy relationships. He isn't ashamed of you, Trevor and Jeff. He loves you and wants to heal this part of your life," Ted assured them.

"Hey, do you remember this guy's name?" Ted asked.

"Um, yeah, I think his name was Brian," Jeff offered, as Trevor nodded his agreement.

"Pick someone to be Brian, would you?" Ted directed.

"James, will you be Brian?" Trevor asked.

"Sure." James stood up and moved to the chair Ted had set in front of Trevor and Jeff.

"Guys, this is what I want you to do. I want you to stand up so you don't feel little anymore. James, you sit here and be Brian. Now guys, tell Brian how what he did impacted you. What did his actions steal from you? How have you felt about yourself since this happened?" Ted directed.

"Ted, this is so weird man. I can't talk to James like he is Brian; besides, it's not that big a deal," Jeff protested.

"I can. I'm pissed and sick and tired of beating myself up and feeling like some sort of freak. I think I am connecting some dots here today. Maybe just a few, but I am wondering if when he gave me a blow job and then asked me to do the same to him if that impacted my curiosity about the same sex?" Trevor said angrily.

"Tell him son. Let him have it," Ted gave permission.

Trevor began, "Brian, you had no right to expose me to sex. I was a kid. I already was living in a nightmare with my mom and dad, and my dad was never there for me. I didn't know up from down and when you did that to me it ignited something in me. A longing for a dad to wrestle with me, hug me, and hold me when I was scared. You ignited in me a man hunger for something I needed, but I didn't have it from my dad. You were someone I looked up to and trusted. You were the cool kid who lived next door. Since I couldn't get my dad's attention, I wanted your attention. But you made it all about sex. Yeah, it turned me on, but I was too young to be turned on. You were wrong, and you should be ashamed of yourself. We were kids!" The veins on Trevor's neck were popping as he pumped his fist into the palm of his hand.

"That's it, Trevor. Let it out. He was wrong—you were a kid. He knew better. You didn't," Ted hurt with him.

"Jeff, how about you?" Ted asked.

"Porn isn't my thing. But girls are, and I think what Brian did…"

Ted stopped him and said, "Talk to him, son. He's right here."

Jeff let out a sharp exhale and then said, "What you did piqued my curiosity and got me started down a trail I shouldn't have gone down. I have talked girls into reenacting what you did to me. I know it's not right. My parents taught me better, but I have felt out of control. I feel guilty, when in reality you are guilty. I feel dirty, when in truth what you did was dirty. You took two innocent kids and exposed them to something they never should have seen, felt, heard, or experienced. It was confusing, and heck, I'm still confused! Sex got all twisted up for me and I shut down some of my feelings. I felt too ashamed to tell my parents, and they are good people. They have asked me over and over if I'm okay. They can tell I haven't been the same since all of that happened. I have kept secrets from the two people who have always loved me. I hate what you did!" Jeff said with snot and tears running down his face.

Ted asked, "Is there more? Is there anything else you need to say to Brian?"

Still standing, both thought for a few minutes, until Trevor said, "Maybe it's okay for me to desire closeness with men, but maybe I don't need to make it about sex. Sex isn't love. I thought it was, but it isn't. Maybe the sexual abuse from you, Brian, felt like it was meeting a need for me: It was affectionate. It was physically close. I liked your body close to mine and to see your muscles ripple—I liked that. But maybe my real need was for *love*. Nothing sexual about it all. Just a human desire to be loved," Trevor pondered aloud.

Ted asked, "Son, can I give you one of those man hugs I gave James earlier today?"

Trevor sort of fell into Ted's arms and Ted just held him like a father with a toddler. Chest to chest. Heart to heart. Man to man. Not a hint of anything sexual. The years of tears released like a flood from the depths of Trevor's being.

Ted just held him and whispered, "That's it. Let it out. Let all of that hurt out, all of that hate for the failures of your dad, the confusion of what Brian ignited in your life. You are not bad, son. You are loveable. You are worthy. You are a delightful son. You are wanted. You are valuable. It's okay to let yourself feel and to have longings. You have longed for a father since before you were born. Father God loves you with all His heart. He wants you for His own. He has been calling your name and seeking your face. He wants a close relationship with you. He wants to be the father you never had. And Trevor, I want to be here for you too." With that, Ted took Trevor's shoulders in his two wrinkled hands and said face to face, eye to eye, "I love you, son."

Trevor couldn't really contain himself. He had never felt such love, but had always hungered for it. James got up from the chair, where he had been playing the role of these two young boys' sexual abuser, and put his arms around Trevor.

"I'm not Brian. I'm James. And I love you too, buddy, and you are no longer alone." Then Jason did the same thing, as did Kevin and lastly Jeff.

"Trevor," Jeff said. "I have felt so much guilt toward you. I knew your home life was hard. I should have told Brian to go to hell and leave us alone. I was such a coward."

"Man, I have felt the same way toward you, Jeff. You were always so innocent and such a good kid. You were everything I wanted to be and so was your family. I always believed, if you hadn't been hanging around me, nothing bad would have happened to you. I thought it was all my fault," Trevor confessed.

"Guys, can you see how it wasn't either one of your fault? Brian was old enough to know better. He was sixteen. And no matter what his story was, he had to know it's never okay to have sex with kids. You were children," James assured them.

Jeff and Trevor nodded, acknowledging they were children, innocent children.

"Good work, gentlemen. This is exactly how we heal. Can you feel it?" Ted asked.

"Yeah, I feel like a dark cloud has lifted for me," Jeff said.

Trevor paused before he said, "Clarity—I feel peaceful—I don't think I have ever felt peaceful. But right now, I feel like the fog has lifted, and maybe, just maybe, there is hope for my life. I also feel a warmth in my chest. What is that?"

"Is it love, son?" Ted asked. "Do you feel loved?"

"I'm not sure. I just feel warm and peaceful. Content," Trevor explained.

"Jesus says He is close to the broken hearted. You have been broken hearted, Trevor. You didn't know your biological parents. And your adoptive parents didn't know how to create a healthy family. You were sexually abused by the neighbor you hoped would be a male role model for you, and you were rejected by your dad. That's a lot for any man to bear, son," Ted comforted him.

"You remind me of King David," Ted said. "His own father called him the worthless one. David confesses in Scripture that both his father and mother abandoned him. He had sexual struggles and I imagine he wondered if he was lovable and if his life had meaning. He also cried out to God and asked Him to forgive the shame of his youth. I often wonder if he experienced sexual abuse of some sort. It's not unusual. And yet God calls him a man after God's own heart. I believe God called him that because David poured his heart out to God on a regular basis. He told God the good, the bad, and the ugly. He expressed anger when he was angry. He expressed sorrow and disappointment. He trusted God with his heart and kept nothing hidden from God, well, almost nothing. When David lustfully took Bathsheba and then killed her husband because she was pregnant with David's child, he tried to keep that a secret, and it ended up being a mess. God wants to know your hurt, your pain, even your secrets, from you. He loves a person who will open up and let Him in. You have done that today with God and with us.

"Son, Trevor, if you surrender your life to Jesus, I think He will do for you what He did for David. David called God, 'The lover of my soul, and the one who walked with me through the valley of death and spread out a banqueting table for me to eat at.' Son, you have walked through some significant pain today. But there is always more. It's never one and done. Become a man like David, a man after God's heart, and your life will be transformed. David suffered tremendous rejection, not just from his own father, but also from his father-in-law who was mentally unstable and frequently jealous of David. If we don't grieve our wounds, surrender the pain and hurt and desire for a pound of flesh, our hearts become hard and we lose our capacity to love. Several times, King Saul threatened and attempted to kill David. And David never pretended it didn't happen; David didn't minimize his painful life experiences. He found a way to grieve the pain and to release the anger he had for the ones who hurt him, so he could keep his heart pure.

"That kind of release isn't for the sake of the other person. It's for the sake of your heart. If you face your pain, grieve it, surrender it to Jesus, you will no longer be the kid who was given up for adoption and not wanted by his adoptive father. You will become the man who is chosen, adopted by God, wanted, and pursued by the Father of all Fathers. If you invite Him in, He will put His royal robe across your shoulders and slip His signet ring onto your finger. He does all this to say, to declare, 'This is my son. He belongs to me. He is my friend and the one I share my secrets with.' You will never be alone again, Trevor. You will belong to God."

"How do I do that?" Trevor asked.

James stepped in, "Trevor, it's pretty straightforward; you just invite Him into your life. Scripture talks about being born again in the spirit. You have been born once, but your spirit hasn't been born again. If you invite Him into your life, your spirit will be born and you will spend eternity with Him. You will never be alone again. Jesus will be your best friend. Well, actually, God the Father, Jesus, and the Holy Spirit will be your three best friends. And then, He says He washes your sin away and makes you white as snow. Jesus went to the cross for our sins. He died so you and I don't have to die. He shed His blood for us, to make us new, to redeem the garbage, to make us new creations in Him. His blood washes us and makes us new men, no longer shackled by our sin and shame."

"I want that. I need that," Trevor said.

"Me too," Jeff echoed.

"I for sure do. I have never felt like a son to anyone either," Kevin stated.

"Well, gentlemen, how about we pray and you can ask Jesus to come into your hearts. Ask Him to cleanse you from sin, and tell Him you want to give him your body, soul, and spirit," Ted said.

"Um, okay," Trevor said as he closed his eyes. "Jesus, my life is a mess. I have felt so alone and like a total failure. If You want me, I am Yours. Come into my life. I open it up to You today. You see it all, all of the secrets, all of the shame. I am asking You to wash me with Your blood and make me a new man." More tears ran down his face.

Kevin jumped in. "Yeah, me too. I would like You to come into my life. Here it is; I am yours. I want You in my life, and I need your help. Help me to become a new man. I'm stuck and can't get myself out of this trap I am caught in. Would You help me?"

Jeff finished with, "God, I was raised to know You. I asked You into my heart when I was six. Do You remember that? I know You do. I walked away from You when the sexual stuff happened with Brian because I was too embarrassed to face You and I figured You were disgusted with me. I didn't think You would want me anymore. But I have missed You. Please forgive me for all of the sexual acting out I did with other girls. I am sorry I treated your daughters like that. I repent. I am back. I am coming home to You today. Wash me clean of the sin and shame." The men moved into the circle with their arms wrapped around each other's necks. It felt like a huddle each man belonged to.

Ted wrapped up with a prayer. "Father, You love these men. You see and know their hearts and You accept them right where they are. You are not ashamed of their sexual brokenness. You are so proud of them for opening up and getting vulnerable and honest. In the Bible, You teach us to confess our sins to one another; sin is missing the mark, and we have all missed the mark. Today, these men did that. I pray You will continue to work out the sexual brokenness in their lives. Hold them tight to Your chest for the rest of their earthly lives. Amen."

MOVING FORWARD

Can sexual tastes be acquired? Our experiences, traumas, and what activates our libido have a profound impact on our sexual tastes. Dopamine is released during a sexual encounter, even an uninvited sexual encounter, which leads to a heightened sense of arousal and sexual craving. The neurotransmitter, dopamine, is responsible for giving us a rush when we accomplish something, so imagine the thrill received when ejaculation is completed.

For Trevor, his first experience was with another man and the release of dopamine reinforced the memory or bonding of the experience, helping the brain to remember where to return for the next arousing encounter. You can imagine how this becomes an addictive cycle and why same-sex porn has become problematic for Trevor. The research on sexual addiction continues to grow, but what we do know is that rather than providing relief for sexual tension, porn delivers tolerance, addictive tendencies, and an eventual decrease in pleasure. This leads the viewer to seek novel thrills, which typically includes an escalation in explicit and graphic materials and some violence.

Ted will be working with the men to reorganize the structure of their brains. Thankfully, God created our brains with the ability for our brain pathways to be rewired and reshaped as we discussed earlier. Scripture refers to this brain rewiring as the transformation of our brain. This happens by not conforming to the pressures and standards of this world. Ted knows, from years of experience that one of the best ways for this to take place is for the men to get into a therapy group where they can practice honesty, receive support, heal from traumas, and practice impulse control through accountability. Some of them will also need individual therapy to work through any trauma or neglect. Some may need treatment for mental health issues such as depression, anxiety, ADHD, mood disorders, and PTSD. I heard Dr. Daniel Amen, a brain disorder specialist, say, "Your brain must be able to cooperate with your recovery."[1]

Recovery is highly possible. Today, we have a much better understanding of addictions and particularly sexual addiction. Sobriety is possible with the willingness to change and given the right help. I believe if a person wants to recover, if they truly are dedicated to healing, if they have hit bottom and are ready to do the work, the right help and resources will appear.

Here are some questions to ponder:

1. Can you see how early sexual experiences create brain problems later in life? What were your formative sexual experiences?
2. How did this story impact you? Are you relating to one of the characters? Who and how?
3. If Ted asked you to talk to someone in the empty chair, who would it be? Why? What happened?
4. Have you connected your sexuality with your spirituality? Or invited Jesus to be a part of this journey? There's no better time than the present.

EIGHT

Time to Heal

Three months had passed and the women continued to meet faithfully. Some days were harder than other days, but having already committed themselves to the group, the women kept at it. Slowly, over time, their stories leaked out, honesty replaced the secrets, and vulnerability became the new normal. They began to notice changes—change within their relationships and change within themselves.

On a side note, some of their stories may shock you. It is shocking to read about the things that have happened to people. My goal isn't to make you feel uncomfortable but to create an honest, open dialogue so we can normalize the need to get the bad out so we can let good in. Stuffing down the bad stuff has been proven to be harmful to our health, our relationships, our mood, and to our personhood. Permission to tell is a vital part of regaining our voice and healing our stories.

Angie had a big breakthrough when she confessed she was having an affair with her daughter's volleyball coach. She confessed to the group that part of the reason she hated her husband and wanted him to disappear was because she had found someone new. Someone who made her feel special. Someone who understood her. He opened up to her and shared with her how miserable he was in his marriage. How his wife never wanted to have sex with him and what started with some casual flirting and feelings of euphoria eventually grew to meeting in secret locations for providing what he wasn't getting at home. Little did Angie consider how she was setting herself up for a relationship that was more about taking than *loving*.

When we struggle with codependency, it's so easy to concentrate our lives on meeting the needs of others, those legitimate and illegitimate needs. People have needs and love is willing to meet those needs, but not at the expense and destruction of a person's soul. Most of us have to struggle with our tendencies to be codependent to someone. We can wear ourselves out trying to act loving instead of being loved. Love focuses on the relational aspect of being with another, not the "What can I do for you or you do for me?"

Don't misunderstand me here. Love is action. Love is a willingness to serve and make sacrifices for the good of the relationship. Jesus warned us about serving two masters. If pleasing people becomes our goal, we become slaves to that person or people, and people can be harsh task masters. Jesus, when Martha was trying to get him to side with her to make her sister Mary help her serve their guests, clearly sided with Mary and said she had chosen what is good and right. Mary chose to sit at Jesus' feet and to soak in His words, His spirit, His character, His way of doing life, His love. It wasn't about proving she was loveable by doing for others. It wasn't taking a *less than* position or adopting a martyr attitude by serving or becoming a slave to another person or group of people. It was about a state of *being*, living in the presence of Jesus, which brings peace, the peace that never comes from busily doing.

I love to make meals, do laundry, and babysit my grandchildren, but none of that has meaning if it isn't done in relationship with my husband, children, and grandchildren. If I serve others because I am afraid of losing their love, or if I am trying to get them to accept me, then I become a slave.

In the same way, if a person has sex with another human to get him or her hooked into a relationship, or to get them to stay, or withholds sex to punish, the motives need to be checked. Sex isn't a weapon to be wielded to get what we want from another person. That is pure and simple manipulation. Sex was never intended to enslave. Sex is meant to be an expression of love.

GROUP WORK

In this chapter, the women in Olivia's group continue to open up and discover more about their own stories. The enemy of our souls wants us to keep our secrets hidden, but as we share our secrets and give a name to our emotions, our brains are healed and rewired.

Through the help of a therapist and group work, these women are able to grieve their losses, sexual traumas, and the impact isolation has made on their lives and relationships.

Being in safe relationships, like the women in Olivia's group, opens our hearts and minds to new beliefs about who we are as sexual creatures. Our sexuality beckons us to face our fear of being known and to grow ourselves into someone capable of loving another and being loved in return. Whatever the state of your sexuality, you can grow and heal. It all begins with you.

Doing grief work in a group is one of the best ways to receive emotional support and to recover losses. God designed us as relational creatures, and we need safe relationships around us in order to heal. Again, rather than tell you, I am going to show you what sharing and openness regarding past trauma looks like in a safe and loving environment.

911

Olivia looked around the circle of women she had grown to love and feel connected to. She sensed they felt the love and healthy attachment grown over the half year they had been meeting together. So much growth had taken place and even Vanessa, the most resistant in the group, opened up in new and vulnerable ways.

Olivia started the group with, "Good afternoon, ladies. Does anyone have a 911? Anything burning that needs to be shared?"

Angie jumped in, "I can't tell you how accepted I felt when I shared my dirty little secret. Thank you for not judging me. I have been judging myself for so long, and I just assumed if you knew the real me, you would run out of the room and never come back. I have hated myself for having an affair. I know it was wrong. I can't believe this is me and my life. I justified my behavior because

I didn't love my husband. But I realized after last week and doing our homework that I had never let him in. I rejected his love from the start. I used him to have kids and then I treated him as if he were disposable. I had no respect for that man. Thank you for not judging the horrible person I have become."

Olivia asked, "Ladies, what do you think? Is Angie horrible?"

In unison, they shook their heads.

Kaycie quietly said, "Angie, how can I judge you when I have pushed James away in different but similar ways? Your sin isn't any different than my sin. And when I heard your story of how your dad was so inappropriate sexually with peeking and leering at you and taking baths with you until you were ten, I understood you. I have grace for you. I have compassion for you. I have empathy for you. And I am so proud of you for finally opening up. I'm praying you will keep trusting us and practicing honesty with us. I don't think you are horrible at all. Please, let us love you so you can heal. And let Jesus love you too."

Tears were flowing freely from the women in the group. Kaycie stood up and gave Angie a long hug. It's true love that heals. The Family of God (FOG) was doing its designated job, healing the wounds of Family of Origin (FOO) so the child within the adult can grow up in healthy ways—surrounded by the love and grace needed to grow a healthy self.

The group paused to soak in what was taking place. Angie had softened and looked like a different woman.

"So, if all this mess hasn't been all my husband's fault, how do I let him in? How do we heal? Is there any chance we can?" Angie pleaded.

"It sounds like you are considering healing your relationship with him," Olivia reflected. "That's a big change, Angie. Do you want to tell us about it?"

"Well, as I started to own my stuff, looking at my own soul, considering my FOO, I realized I have had a big part in the breakdown of this marriage. From our honeymoon, I was guarded and didn't want to let a man close to me. I shut him out as much as he shut me out. And I've hurt him, maybe even more than he hurt me. He wanted sex with me, but I rejected him and had sex with another man. I have to take full responsibility for that. Our children love him and he is a good provider. He never attached to his mother and I'm sure he is just very anxious in his attachment style and it comes across as needy and clingy. With my avoidant style it has only polarized us."

Olivia said, "It sounds like you read the book I recommended about attachment."

"Yes, Dr. Sue Johnson's book has been life changing for me. I can see my part and realize Dylan and I don't have to keep hunting the bad guy. We can become aware of our attachment styles and work to connect instead of disconnect," Angie stated.

"Wow, Angie, big growth!" The women noted.

"How does that feel?" Olivia asked.

"It feels hopeful. If I take responsibility for my part, I am empowered to grow and change. If all I ever do is blame him, I am stuck and feel anything but empowered. We are actually moving toward each other. And I think I know what my next step is," she stated.

Emily asked, "So what's your next step?"

"I have to come clean with him about the affair. I broke it off with the volleyball coach the week after I told you all about it. I admit, it was hard to do though. It was the best, most exciting sex I have ever had, but it was also the most shaming thing I have ever done. I can't keep living with secrets. This group has taught me my secrets are keeping me sick; and I am sick and tired of being sick and tired. I am ready to live without shame. How do I tell him? What if he leaves me? What about the kids?" Angie wondered aloud.

"Tell him like you told us, Angie," Betty advised. "Tell him you are sad you shut him out from the very start. Tell him you are sad you and he haven't moved toward each other but moved away emotionally and physically. Then tell him you have broken off this relationship and you want to start over with him if he will have you. Tell him you are deeply sorry for hurting him and for being unfaithful to him. Isn't that what every spouse wants to hear, when your spouse has been sexually unfaithful?" Betty asked.

"Betty, what about you? Where is your relationship with your husband?" Olivia asked.

Betty's face darkened and she looked down at her hands. "Well—more secrets have come out." Her voice broke. "He has abused more children than I ever dreamed possible. Now, I'm living with my own guilt and shame. I was so stupid and didn't protect these children—my own grandchildren—from him. I am so ashamed." Tears of regret streamed from her closed eyes, as she sobbed.

Two women got up from their chairs and stood behind Betty to give her comfort and support.

"That's so hard, Betty, and I hurt like heck for you. But I am also so proud of you for no longer being in denial, and, instead of being a part of the problem, you are now a part of the solution. That's huge, Betty," Mary Francis said.

Taking in the women's acceptance, Betty dried her tears and hugged the ladies circled around her.

She continued, "He, most likely, is going to prison. I think I am going to need to divorce him to show my children and grand-children that I will never again tolerate sexual abuse of a child. He has proven that children are not safe around him. Divorce is against every value I have held dear, but human life has become a higher value for me." She said this with a newfound confidence, as she dried her eyes with a tissue.

The women celebrated her courage and honesty.

Mary Francis said, "I grieve with you for the loss of your marriage and the man you thought you married. That's a loss for you, Betty. I'm so sorry." Mary Francis paused for a moment and then continued nervously, "I'm not sure if Todd and I are going to make it—I had such high hopes, but he dropped out of his recovery group, is drinking again, and he came home with lipstick on his collar and smelt like Chanel No. 5, at three o'clock in the morning. I asked him to sleep on the couch, which he knows is our safety plan agreement, but he got belligerent and said I could go sleep out in the doghouse before he was sleeping on the couch. He yelled at me, hollering that he was the one paying the rent and if I didn't like his drinking and carousing then I was welcome to leave. He shoved me against the wall and then passed out on the bed. I cried most of the night. I'm not sure I have much of a choice except to separate from him and tell him that he has to be in recovery if there is any hope for us at all."

All eyes had shifted from Betty to Mary Francis. You could feel the shared grief. Emily reached out and put her arms around Mary Francis.

"Oh, Mary Francis, that is terrible. I'm so sad he has relapsed," Kaycie said. "Did he hurt you when he shoved you into the wall? Has he done that before? Do you and the kids need a place to stay?"

"Thanks, let me think about what my next move will be. Yes, he has pushed me before and slapped me a few times, but I usually deserve it," Mary Francis said.

"Mary Francis, do you deserve to be slapped and shoved?" Olivia asked.

"Well, I can get real mouthy and, typically, if he hits me, I hit him back," she quietly responded.

"Can you give the emotion you are feeling a label or a name?" Olivia asked.

"I feel sad, and broken, and lost, and unlovable..." She sobbed.

"Mary Francis—I don't know what to say, but I do know you are lovable," Holly reminded her.

"Am I lovable?" Mary Francis asked, her eyes pleaded.

"You are wondering if you have value, if you are worth loving," Olivia stated.

"Yes, I need to know if there is something fundamentally wrong with me and if I am too broken for someone to love me for me—not for my big breasts, not for my long blonde hair, not for my willingness to put out. Just me," Mary Francis stated.

"What do you think, Mary Francis? Are you lovable?"

After a long pause, Mary Francis wiped a tear off her cheek and responded, "Yes. Yes, I am." She said, "I can look around this room and see I am lovable. And I am going to love me even if Todd decides not to." Her shoulders relaxed with her last words.

A deep sigh of celebration and relief for Mary Francis was released. The women supporting her had a sense she would make it.

"Please, let us know how we can support you through this, Mary Francis. We do love you and you aren't alone anymore," Olivia responded.

WHAT'S IT ALL ABOUT?

During the many months together, the women experienced marriages healing, attachment breaches mending, and personal growth happening. They celebrated the victories, the good, the new, but they also learned how to grieve the sad and negative realities of life. Today they grieved with Betty and Mary Francis, while celebrating these two women's newfound strength.

The group was silent for a few moments to honor the sadness they all felt.

"Not to totally change the topic," Kaycie said, "and I don't want to be insensitive to what you two women are going through right now, but I have a big question."

"What is it, Kaycie?" Olivia asked.

"Okay, so what is healthy sex anyway? What does it look like when two people who love each other and love God make love? I really want to know."

The women looked at Olivia, hoping she would answer the question. They were completely curious, given how twisted sex had been for this particular group of women.

Olivia looked around at the ladies to make sure everyone was on the same page before she answered Kaycie's question. "Well, we have to remember sex is God's idea. He is the creator of human sexuality and declared everything He made was good. His intention was for sex to bond a man and woman to one another in a covenantal relationship—a relationship that provides sexual safety. He never intended for sex to be used as a weapon of violence, or dominance, or anger, or hurt. I am sure God grieves deeply for what we humans have done with this most exquisite of gifts and for what you women have been through. Again, He never intended for us to have experienced sexual trauma.

"God created sex to be a way for us to intimately connect with our spouse. He gave females lips, breasts, a clitoris, labia majora and minora, and a vagina. He also created a very sensitive zone, which if she were wearing short shorts would describe that area from her waist to her vagina, and, on the other side, from her waist down her buttocks and down to the perineum. In the Song of Solomon, the woman says, 'Awake, north wind! Rise up, south wind! Blow on my garden and spread its fragrance all around. Come into your garden, my love; taste its finest fruits' (Song of Sol. 4:16; NLT).

"Talk about permission given to enjoy and validate female sexual desire! This is written in God's word, and it is the woman speaking. She is recognizing that her brain, located on the north pole of her body, is her biggest sex organ. She is asking the wind to blow over her brain so she can clear her head. Women tend to have busy brains and I think she is acknowledging she needs God's help with her sexual hang-ups, whatever those are. She prays for help to allow her mind to focus on sexual thoughts and having sex with her husband. This is also a commentary of female sexuality.

"The female brain has to feel safe in order for her to relax enough to enjoy sex. Think about it: females are more vulnerable than males when it comes to sex. Men are stronger and bigger and that fact alone can feel physically threatening to a woman. She can fear getting pregnant, knowing that a pregnancy requires so much more from her than it does her male partner. She also knows her path to sensuality is slower than her husband's. Females need much more emotional connection, talking, caressing, and time to get into desire and arousal than men typically do.

"The woman in the Song of Songs goes on to say, 'Rise up, south wind! Blow on my garden' (NLT). The south wind is warm and inviting. She wants to warm up and get things enlivened in her garden, which is a reference to her clitoris, labia majora and labia minora, and vagina. She wants to experience sexual desire and to feel the wetness of arousal and the fragrance that is released from a woman's body when she is sexually ready. The woman in Song of Songs 4:16 then says, 'Oh, let my lover enter his garden! Yes, let him eat the fine, ripe fruits.' This sounds like a reference to intercourse and perhaps oral sex and the many delectable ways they enjoy her garden together. And this is all possible when her brain and her body work together, in a safe context.

"Besides safety, I think the next biggest thing for women is to give themselves permission to be sexual and to fully enjoy the pleasure God intended her to have. If God was the prude that so many make Him out to be, He definitely wouldn't have given females a clitoris. The clitoris is a sensitive bundle of nerve endings, designed for sexual pleasure and the key to female orgasm. It is similar to the male penis, but unique in that it contains over eight thousand nerve endings. A clitoris isn't necessary for reproduction. And He could have made sexual intercourse strictly for reproducing. But He clearly didn't. Instead, He made sex for pleasure and attachment, as well as for reproducing offspring. He made it possible for couples to enjoy many varieties of sexual pleasure, from a foot rub and body massage, to discovering the over three hundred erogenous zones on a woman's body, kissing, caressing, breast stimulation, manual and oral play, and intercourse.

PROCESS TIME

Kaycie raised her hand, signaling to Olivia that she had a question. Olivia paused and Kaycie hesitantly asked, "So I feel embarrassed to ask this, but what about oral sex? I'm not sure I am a good sexual partner because I don't really like oral sex. Sometimes I even worry I am depriving James."

"Tell me more, Kaycie?" Olivia asked.

"Well, I don't feel comfortable with it. I think it's a trigger for me," Kaycie said.

"What does it trigger for you, Kaycie?" Olivia wondered aloud.

"Well, I don't have any specific memories, just shadows and feelings," Kaycie acknowledged.

"That sounds really normal, Kaycie. Most people have fragmented memories about something that might have happened to them. Do you have any ideas about what might have happened?" Olivia asked.

"After Dad left, Mom dated a guy who was a real jerk. I think he may have done oral sex on me." Kaycie shuddered.

"Kaycie, I'm so sorry. No wonder you get triggered," Olivia empathized.

"Yeah, it was scary for me. I almost want to throw up just thinking about it," Kaycie admitted, her eyes downcast.

"Yes, that was scary. Have you allowed yourself to grieve what was done to you?" Olivia asked.

"No, this is the first time I have said it to anyone," Kaycie admitted.

"I feel sick he would do that to you," Mary Francis validated. "No wonder you don't like oral sex."

"Yeah, it makes sense now," Kaycie reflected.

"Would it be helpful if I shared how my husband and I worked through some of this?" Olivia asked the women. Olivia never wanted the group to be about her but about and for the women in the group. But sometimes a personal example can be therapeutic.

The women unanimously said *yes*.

"You may remember how I shared at the beginning I experienced sexual abuse? Well, oral was part of that. So, it really triggered me. I finally realized the most helpful thing I could do was explain that to my husband. I just told him that it triggered me.

And he totally understood, and my honesty invited his. He shared with me how a friend of his older sisters would sneak into his room and perform oral sex on him in the middle of the night.

"We both shared our shameful experiences with each other and prayed God would redeem those memories and experiences for us. No pressure, no shame, and lots of grace. One of the most healing things my husband did for me was when we were making love and something triggered me—I would stop and ask him to hold me. He would, and then he would pray for me. I felt safe with him. I figured if a man would stop in the middle of making love and hold me and pray for me that I was safe with him. That feeling of safety has helped us become freer sexually with each other. What was once a taboo no longer is.

"But here's the important thing. There are no *should*s when it comes to making love, other than it should be mutually pleasurable. There are lots of ways to have fun together, and, if you don't like oral sex, don't feel like you have to do it to be a good lover. But don't shut out the idea either. Try to work through the trigger and then you can possibly re-frame it. What I mean by that is oral sex started as something shameful and confusing and scary for me, but once I understood that what happened was abuse, I could grieve what happened to me. I could then sort through what was bad and what was good. Sexual abuse is always bad, but making love with a husband who loves you is good.

"Does that help? Please, always feel like you can ask me anything," Olivia said.

"Yes, that helps a lot," Kaycie responded. "I feel less pressured about sexually performing and like something is wrong with me if I don't feel comfortable with oral sex. You are saying it's okay for James and me to figure out what works for us and what we like and don't like sexually. And I don't need to feel any shame for something I don't like or want to do, right?"

"Yes, Kaycie, you two figure out what is right for you," Olivia reassured.

STAYING OPEN

Olivia continued, "God is a creative artist and when it comes to human sexuality, I think He wants us to be creative and imaginative. Sex between a husband and wife is completely *unique* to that couple. Every couple has the right to figure out what they consider pleasurable and take into consideration one another's personal preferences. No one should force or pressure another person into anything. It's important we hear one another's 'No!' and respect it. But it's also important that we stay open. It is normal for humans to desire sex; there's nothing wrong with that."

Kaycie responded, "So, for James and me sex started out on a drug-induced high. We felt attraction, but that was about it. I wanted his attention and he probably just wanted an orgasm. How do we redeem that beginning?"

"Kaycie, everything is redeemable in God's kingdom. Everything. I think especially sexuality. He gives several examples of some of His most powerful people making a mess of sex and how He redeemed it.

"Sarah threw her handmaiden, Hagar, at Abraham, and told him to make a baby with her. He complied. It was a jealous mess to say the least, but God redeemed it and gave them Isaac, when they had zero capacity to conceive a child.

"There are other biblical examples of God's children who made a mess of sex because they hadn't tied sex to emotional connection. Scripture says Adam knew his wife Eve. This is a term for *yada*, a Hebrew word meaning to know and to be known. Adam had a knowing relationship with Eve. She was much more than a sexual object to him. Scripture says David lay with Bathsheba. This was strictly a sexual act, motivated by lust. There was zero emotional connection. But God redeemed sex for these biblical examples.

"He surely wants to do the same for each of us. God loves to do the impossible for us. He loves to do the improbable and the highly unlikely. It's never too late and we are never too far gone. There is hope for every one of us, no matter what our sexual history has been or currently is. Nothing is outside His grace and love and redemptive power. Nothing.

"Next month I am teaching a weekend seminar on healthy sexuality. I would love for you ladies to attend, and if you would like to, you can invite your husbands and friends. It will be fun," Olivia reassured them.

"We will be there," Kaycie said, smiling.

"I may come with or without Todd," Mary Francis said.

"It would be great for Dylan and me, but we'll see if he is still around or if he has decided to leave me by then. Sex has never been great with us—so awkward. Honestly, I can have some grace for him about his temptation with porn. Maybe if that part of our lives were better, we might have more love to share with each other," Angie commented.

"Well, not me. I am still so mad at Evan," said Emily. "I just don't know if I can ever move past my anger. I can't let it go that he was chatting with a naked woman online and doing God only knows what. Seriously, how do I get past that? It's glued in my memory! Whenever I close my eyes, I feel sick thinking about what they were doing online together. How sexy he talked to her—it's just all so dirty now. I don't think I can ever see sex as a gift from God—that just seems like the biggest joke in the world to me now. It hasn't been a gift for us; it's been a curse."

Holly said, "Em, it's been really broken for you and Evan. It has been for Joe and me as well. I hear you about the images. Joe and I watched porn together, thinking it would spice things up for us, and it did at first. But then we lost the connection sex was meant to bring to us and we started lusting for more and different and, man, it got messed up. I hurt with you, Emily. I want this to be better for all of us. I want to have the kind of sex God wants for us.

"But, just like you, I have no idea how Joe and I are going to go from some pretty kinky stuff—to having sacred sex? That just sounds way too holy for us. Is sex really redeemable? I mean—we have been doing this stuff for over ten years and just a year ago, we had a threesome and it got really crazy. The other woman we let into our bed became jealous and wanted me out of the picture. She tried her best to split Joe and me up. It was a huge wake-up call for me.

"We became believers in Christ around that time and one day we were reading our Bibles together and it said in Hebrews 13:4, 'Honor marriage, and guard the sacredness of sexual intimacy between wife and husband. God draws a firm line against casual and illicit sex.' Right then, we realized we had not guarded our sexual intimacy, and we sure hadn't treated it as sacred—sex was anything but sacred. We were completely casual about it and we engaged in lots of illicit sex. Our pastor told us God wants to be part of every detail of our lives. Of course, we didn't bring up what we were doing sexually, but we assumed if the pastor said God wanted to be involved in every detail of our lives, then why not the sexual part? So, we started praying and that's when we heard about this women's group and the men's group. We signed up as fast as we could and here we are today."

Holly continued, a little relieved, "So, yeah, we will be there, Olivia. Sign us up today. We want this redeemed and I am old enough to know it's not going to change on its own. Joe and I are both going to have to do our parts to make this new."

Emily closed her eyes and said, "Okay, I will try. I will try to let go of my rage. I will try to let go of punishing Evan forever for his stupidity—I'll try to let things change."

"Emily, that's big. What does it feel like to even say that?" Angie asked.

"I can feel myself resisting, even as I say it."

"Resistance is all around us, ladies. We all face resistance on a daily basis. It's everywhere. Resistance wants to keep every one of us stuck, and resistance causes us to keep our walls up and we think these walls will protect us, while they only keep love and joy and goodness out. So you are normal, Emily," Olivia said.

"Who else is feeling resistant?" Olivia asked the group.

"Me..." Vanessa said.

"Would you like to tell us more, Vanessa?" Olivia offered.

"I have a porn and masturbation issue. My husband left me because he said I never want him anymore. He was right; my vibrator was way more satisfying. And I think I am pretty hooked on porn. It's become a habit, and I can't shake it. I think about leaving here and going home to watch a little porn and spending time with my best friend called vibrator. Heck, I don't even know how to relate to a real man anymore," she blurted out.

"What's that like for you? It sounds lonely, Vanessa," Kaycie wondered aloud.

"It is—I am dying inside. Numb. I read one romance novel after another and wonder why I am so alone. I almost couldn't take it the other night and so I got on Craigslist, pondering a one-night stand with a complete stranger. I feel out of control sexually. I'm so alone, but one part of me likes it," Vanessa confessed.

Kaycie was sitting next to her and moved in a little closer. "Your secret doesn't freak me out. I have wondered why you were so quiet for so long. Is there anything else you want us to know?"

"No, I think that's it. Except, I really miss my husband. It's so quiet in the house, and I am sick of frozen pizza, romance novels, and, mostly, being alone. I don't think he would ever come back to me. I couldn't even ask him to. He hasn't moved on. He just moved out and told me I had to get help. I have sat here for six months frozen. Afraid to tell you women I am the one with what feels like a sexual addiction. I am the one with the porn issue. I am the one who masturbates at least twice a day, sometimes more. What is wrong with me?" Vanessa asked with frustration.

Olivia asked, "Vanessa, you have heard us talk about how sexual addiction isn't about sex, but about medicating pain or stress. What are you medicating?"

"I can't even talk about it. It's so bad," Vanessa said flatly.

"It seems too dark to talk about," Olivia reflected.

"Yes. It was so bad—so awful. And I am such a slut. I'm not good enough to have relationships or have people care about me. I couldn't tolerate my husband wanting to have a relationship with me. I was ruined in college," Vanessa revealed.

"Can you tell us about it, Vanessa, what ruined you?" Olivia asked gently.

"I was a college athlete and at a big tournament with both male and female athletes. Both teams had big wins that day and we were all celebrating afterward, at a local pub. I was at the bar with several of the other girls, when a couple of the male athletes approached us; one of the guys I knew well, and actually dated.

"Somewhere in the conversation the other girls went to the bathroom. I think one of the male athletes slipped something into my drink—next thing you know, I am at an apartment, and all three of these guys are having sex with me. I started to sober up and they wouldn't stop. I begged them to stop. But they wouldn't listen. They did unspeakable things to me, and, if I remember right, several other guys joined in as well.

"They raped me for hours, said the filthiest things to me imaginable, and forced me to have oral sex with them. I have never told anyone—ever. I went numb after that, but for some reason developed a habit of masturbation mixed with porn and sometimes I do it so hard it hurts. I realize I'm self abusing. But I blame myself for what happened and I'm filled with so much self-hatred. See, I am so screwed up! I don't think there is any hope for me to be normal. I was ruined."

The women had tears in their eyes with some streaming down already tear-streaked cheeks.

"Oh, Vanessa," Kaycie said. "I can't tell you how much I hurt for you! I am so sorry you were drugged and raped. I am so sad for how you took what they did to you and blamed yourself and thought you were ruined. You aren't ruined, and it wasn't your fault. You aren't to blame for their behavior. I work in college ministry and, sadly, things like this happen far more than any of us could imagine. But I want you to know, you aren't alone anymore. Your story is safe here. Please keep telling us your story. I believe you."

"Well, my performance as an athlete was shot after that. I couldn't concentrate, and the nightmares were so bad I had to go on anti-depressant, anti-anxiety, and sleeping pills. That wasn't enough, so I started drinking. Then I needed more relief so that's when I discovered porn and masturbation helped calm the anxiety for a while. It was such a vicious cycle I eventually dropped out of school.

"I was pre-med and on an athletic and academic scholarship, at a top-notch school. My dad is a doctor and so was his dad. I was in line to follow in his footsteps. Life looked so full of promise and hope and then in one night everything changed for me. You may wonder why I didn't turn them in—well—my family is very high profile and wealthy. They had great hopes for their only child to be successful. I had been sleeping with one of the athletes, and I just knew if I reported it to the police, they would make it sound like I wanted it, that I was some sort of slut, and they would have ruined me and my family. At least that's the story I created in my head and lived in fear of."

"A sexual assault is so shaming for the victim," Olivia acknowledged. "Your story is safe here, Vanessa."

"Thank you for telling us your story. I know that took courage many people never find. You are very brave. And being honest takes lots of courage. Is there anything else you want us to know?" Olivia asked.

"Yes, one more thing. I contracted an STD and, because it was one that didn't have any noticeable side effects, I didn't have it treated early enough. Now—I can't have any children." With this last revelation, Vanessa let out a sob that sounded more like a howl. From the depths of her being, she let the sorrow flow. The tears she held in for over a decade were released like a broken dam flooding the earth.

FINAL THOUGHTS

There is a lot to process from this chapter. Bringing darkness into the light takes enormous courage. Olivia completely understood why Vanessa had been a nearly *silent* member of the group for so long. Olivia would regularly invite Vanessa to share, but it wasn't until this point in the group process that Vanessa felt safe. It takes time and patience for people to tell their stories. Typically, the darker the story, the harder it is to tell and the more resistance there is to telling it.

You can see how Vanessa would be tempted to drive her husband away. And how living in isolation and meeting her own sexual needs would be so much safer for her than being vulnerable with a man. I wonder if she made an inner vow to never let another man hurt her the way she was hurt in college. It's easy to have empathy for her when we understand her story and the trauma she went through. The amount of shame she experienced would send most of us into hiding—that's what shame does. It screams, "Isolate, take care of yourself. Don't let others in." Because of the traumatic sexual assault, she became more and more isolated. And isolation leads to depression and despondency. As stated earlier, we are relational creatures by design.

It took tremendous amounts of courage for Vanessa to open up and it took her six months to feel safe. We live in an instant society. We pace in front of the microwave, and want the ITM machine to work faster. We are a hurried and rushed society. But *hurry up* doesn't create lasting relationships. You can tell from these women's stories, relationship is what harmed them, but relationship is also what is healing them. This is as God designed; none of us can go it alone. Our brains will register "risk" when we are about to share. Most resist this "risk" and never open up. They hide and justify it with the thought emotions are silly and they just need to get over what happened. I think this is why Jesus said the gate is narrow and few will enter it.

Experts say only one out of ten people who receive helpful information or opportunities for growth will actually apply what they learn to their personal lives. Growth isn't easy or automatic and one of my biggest concerns for the body of Christ is our *passive* rescue wishes. We pray God will change something or rescue us from something bad or hard, but we never apply ourselves to the situation. Then we get mad at God for "not showing up for me."

God never promised to be our magic genie. I love what Dallas Willard says, "Grace is not opposed to effort, it is opposed to earning. Earning is an attitude. Effort is an action."[1] We don't need to do a thing to earn His love, His attention, or His grace. But we do need to apply ourselves to the health and wholeness of our own lives and that takes effort.

Olivia and the other women in the group could feel hope rising, as the women gave labels to their emotions through telling their stories. You have to give negative emotions a name. In one MRI study, appropriately titled "Putting Feelings into Words" participants viewed pictures of people with emotional facial expressions. Predictably, each participant's amygdala activated to the emotions in the picture. But when they were asked to name the emotion, the ventrolateral prefrontal cortex activated and reduced the emotional amygdala reactivity.

In other words, consciously recognizing the emotions reduced their impact. Hiding or stuffing our emotions doesn't work. Neuroscientists have found that people who tried to suppress a negative emotional experience failed to do so. While they thought they looked fine outwardly, inwardly their limbic system was just as aroused as without suppression, and, in some cases, even more aroused. Kevin Ochsner, at Columbia, repeated these findings using fMRI. Working hard to keep negative emotions under wraps doesn't work and typically backfires.[2]

I ask people who are experiencing an emotion to give it a name. Typically, giving it one or two names is the most impactful. Stopping to label an emotion reduces the arousal in the limbic system by activating your prefrontal cortex. It helps people who are recalling a trauma memory to calm their nervous system and get back into their smart brain (the prefrontal cortex or the governor of the brain), not wanting them to get stuck in the emotionally fired up amygdala. Becoming whole is a process of defining and giving names to what we think, feel, and want. It's a process of healthy self-differentiating our thinking from our emotions. This is the process group work helps with.

I know that reading some of these stories can feel heavy, shocking, sad. Here is the truth: as these women tell their stories, label their emotions, and become honest with others in a safe place, they are healing their trauma. Trauma is bad, and I never want to minimize the horrible things we humans do to one another, but we must remember there is so much hope.

God created us to heal. He created our brains to rewire. He gave us neuroplasticity; our brain wiring isn't rigid. If we practice and participate in healing—healing takes place. Healing is less about the actual trauma and more about whether we are willing to engage in the healing process. I believe with all of my heart that, if we engage in the process, the process will work for us. I want to encourage you not to waste your story and to not let your story define you. Where you are today isn't where you will have to be tomorrow if you will make the decision to engage in the process. Here are some questions for you to process before moving on to the next chapter.

MOVING FORWARD

1. Label and name the emotion you are experiencing right now. Are you sad? Mad? Disgusted?

2. Explore your own level of resistance. On a scale of one to ten (ten being highly resistant), how resistant are you to entering into the healing process? Why?

3. Are you shocked by the amount of sexual abuse these women experienced? It is shocking, but it is a reality. Are you willing to face this reality? Look at your own history? Become an advocate for those who have experienced sexual trauma? Become a part of the solution?

4. Take a few moments and invite God to search your heart to see if there is any unfinished business concerning your sexual history.

5. Invite God into any memory and to lead you in the healing process.

NINE

Sexual Wholeness Seminar

PART I: MORNING SESSION

The truth is most adults have never had anyone talk with them about human sexuality. Most people do not receive a healthy sexual education. Many issues and problems can be resolved through biblical sex education and having someone or a group of safe people to talk things through with. This is Olivia's goal for this intensive seminar. She is hoping to create a dialogue for people to learn, ask questions, and to process their own issues.

Her prayer is the isolation of sexual shame will be broken and people will find God's healing and redemption through open and honest conversations around the topic. She has witnessed it many times and prays today will be another day of guiding a group into a deeper connection with themselves, others, and God, through the topic of sex.

As Olivia reflects, she is grateful for the hard work she has done in partnership with God, in the process of recovering her own soul from the abyss of sexual abuse. She wouldn't change a thing about her history, believing wholeheartedly her history is now God's history and he has permission to use her story for good. At the least, she knows she could not invite people to go places she refused to go. She is happy she said "Yes" so many years ago.

Olivia gathered her group of volunteers to pray for the weekend seminar. There was excitement in the room, as they prepared for the people to start streaming in.

"Thank you all for coming today and for lending your support. I know you have been and continue to be on your own sexual healing journey. And it's exciting for me to watch your growth and to know you want to give back to others what you have experienced. Thank you for caring about the people who will be here and attuning to what his or her needs will be. When we talk about human sexuality, it can stir all kinds of emotions and, with it, lots of shame. Many of the people coming are in the recovery process of sexual addiction. Some are coming because they have experienced abuse and some have sexual struggles. Let's pray before everyone arrives.

"Father, You are a good, good God, and we thank You for what You have done in our lives and for this time we have today to talk about a topic dear to Your heart. We only see and understand in part, so we pray for your wisdom, insight, and understanding concerning human sexuality. We pray hearts will be open, for your protection over those who carry trauma and shame around this topic, and for you to heal those who need healing. Redeem this topic in your children's lives. Amen."

Men and women started filling the room, some single, some couples, some looking happy and excited, others looking anxious and afraid. Purposefully, the leaders greeted each person and did their best to make people feel welcome and comfortable.

Olivia started with a welcome and then explained, "Depending on the way we were raised, we can have many different emotions about being here. Some of you may be thinking, *Finally, we are going to talk about this in an adult, constructive way.* Others are thinking, *Is this necessary? I feel extremely uncomfortable; I never have understood what the big deal is about sex. Can't we just ignore it and it will all go away?*

"A few of you may be thinking, *This is really a dark topic for me and nothing good has come from this topic—only pain and sorrow.* If that is you, I hurt with you. This topic can bring up many different emotions for people. I think that's why I am passionate about having these types of conversations, creating opportunities for us to have healthy dialogues around an often taboo topic. Thank you for being present today. We have a group of trained volunteers who are here to listen and give you support.

"Let's start with a question, who taught you about sex?" Olivia asked the group.

"My mom had the talk with me about the birds and bees when I was thirteen," Emily, the woman from Olivia's group, offered.

"That's good. How was that for you? Was it helpful?" Olivia asked.

"Yes and no," Emily said. "Yes, in that it answered my questions about where babies come from and how they get here. I learned the 'functions' of sex. But, in our relationship," she said, pointing to the husband she didn't think would want to come, "we don't need help with the how, but the *why* and the *what*. Why is sex important? What is the purpose? What creates a great married sex life? Why work at it? Why bother when it is broken? And why not just let it die or move on?" Emily wondered aloud.

Olivia smiled. "Emily, your questions, and wonderings are valid. You have brought up questions I am sure many in this room would like answers for." As Olivia scanned the room, she saw heads nodding.

"God designed sex, and, when He created mankind, He wired sexuality into our system. Obviously, for reproducing offspring, but when we really stop and consider how He designed us, you see a work of art, and He is the creative genius. We also know everything God created He said was good, with one exception. He declared it wasn't good for mankind to be alone, so He put us into relationships. These relationships have the potential to be communal as well as sexual. But the Fall of mankind brought lots of misery to our capacity for relationships. Our father and mother, Adam and Eve, chose to sin, and sin leads to shame, and shame leads to hiding. I think we have been hiding in shame ever since then. It never was God's plan and it still isn't. He even sent His Son to redeem everything that was lost, broken, and stolen from his children—including our sexuality.

"Proverbs 6:20–23 says, 'Good friend, follow your father's good advice; don't wander off from your mother's teachings.' I think one of the biggest problems with our sexuality is our fathers and mothers didn't teach us much about this very important part of who we are; truthfully, neither have our spiritual mothers and fathers.

"Baby Boomers ushered in the Sexual Revolution and opened wide the doors to sexual immorality. We see the consequences of this generation: divorce has escalated significantly from our parents' generation; infidelities; STDs have skyrocketed; sexual addiction is on the rise; unwanted pregnancies; not to mention the heartbreak and heartache that comes with a lack of sexual boundaries. Besides Emily, did anyone else receive sexual instructions from their parents?"

Everyone looked around the room, one other hand raised and, much like Emily's mother, a father had *the talk* with his son.

"So, where did the rest of you learn about sex?" Olivia asked.

"Well, porn has been a big teacher for me and the locker room. I was curious, and a friend told me porn would teach me everything I needed to know," a young man offered from the back of the room.

Olivia asked the group, "How many of you can identify with what he just said?"

Many hands raised and heads nodded.

"Porn has been normalized in the world we live in. It's available twenty-four seven. Before the internet, people had to leave their homes and go purchase pornographic materials. Now it's a click away.

"Daily, I see the struggles porn has caused in people's lives. Women caught in the web of masturbation, porn, and romance novels, or online sexual relationships. People are confused about gender because they have watched same-sex porn and now it has shaped their tastes in ways they can't make sense of. Men distraught over their sexual habits, feeling enslaved to images on a screen. Wives hurt because they feel rejected, as though they have lost their husbands to porn. Husbands who no longer make love to their wives because it has become easier to have sex with an image on the other side of a computer screen.

"We call it *autosex,* which means to have sex with yourself. God's plan for sexuality was that our desire for sex would draw us into relationship with another. Our sexuality would cause us to be drawn deeper into intimacy with God and another—into a depth of connection where we are known and knowing another. His intention was never for sex to leave us lonely and ashamed, but for it to leave us connected and loved and filled with joy.

"Our culture has twisted this topic to the point where we think abnormal is normal and normal is abnormal. We call what is bad for us good and what is good for us bad or boring. Let me give you a few up-to-date statistics to help you grasp the problem porn is:

1. One in ten American males (thirteen and older) views porn daily.
2. Half use it monthly or more often.
3. One in five comes across porn daily, even if they're not looking for it.
4. Less than half consider viewing pornography as wrong.
5. Eight out of ten of those who view porn use online videos (81 percent); half use online pictures (49 percent).

6. One percent of American females, ages thirteen and older, use porn daily; seven percent use it weekly.

7. Sixty-eight percent of porn users say they are comfortable with how much they use porn.

"The top five reasons both males and females say they use porn is:

1. For personal arousal
2. Curiosity
3. Boredom
4. To get tips or ideas for my own sex life
5. It's just fun[1]

"For Christians, they are twice as likely as all others to feel a sense of guilt when they use porn (34 percent vs. 15 percent) and say they are currently trying to stop using porn (19 percent vs. 7 percent). Married adults are three times more likely than single adults to say porn sometimes hurts their relationships (6 percent vs. 2 percent) and that they are currently trying to stop using porn (10 percent vs. 3 percent). Forty-two percent of single adults who use porn say none of the people in their lives know about their porn use (compared to 27 percent of married adults).

"Porn addiction is ultimately an intimacy disorder. People who are more avoidant in their attachment style may find closeness with another person uncomfortable. It can be much easier to bond with a virtual sex partner because there is no need for intimacy. Many sex addicts end up depriving their spouses or partners of sexual intimacy for three reasons: 1) They have difficulty achieving an erection or otherwise having intercourse without the constant visual stimulation pornography provides. 2) They have already masturbated and taken care of themselves while using porn. 3) There is nothing left to give to their spouse, leaving the spouse feeling very alone.[2]

"These issues lead to low self-esteem, comparisons, and depression. Again, God created us for human connections and when a person is deprived of that relationship, especially in a marriage, it leads to an attachment protest—anger, clinging, depression, and eventually detachment—as it rightly should. I think, naively and foolishly, the Baby Boomers didn't really think through their sexual choices or the impact those choices would have on the generations to follow. There was little understanding of neuroscience and the impact sexuality has on the brain. We certainly didn't understand neurochemicals. Now we know pornography changes our brains, and frequent use of porn damages the relational, courting center of our brain. It's no wonder fewer and fewer Americans are marrying, and, when they do, they are doing so at a much later age.

"Sexual boredom is cited repeatedly as a reason for using porn. It's true porn is highly arousing, but the question has to be asked, *What is it arousing you to?* The images on the screen are arousing you, not your spouse, or another human being. This is why the porn user eventually stops making love to their spouse; he or she doesn't arouse them anymore. Their sexual appetites have been reshaped by porn. What once was arousing is no longer a turn-on. A man making love to his wife has now become boring and dull; it has for her as well. Sex for this couple has become mostly mechanical, if they have sex at all. There can be intercourse and orgasm, but with little emotional connection; so sex becomes uninteresting and passion dies.

"Making love to another person requires curiosity and exploration. When porn has filled that need, lovemaking becomes more of a chore. Porn will eventually become boring as well, in the sense that porn is completely selfish and about getting what one wants, a quick release, or a turn-on, and it nullifies the true meaning and complexity of sex with another human being.

"This is why the images continue to get more degrading, cruel, and violent, the need for the *high* porn provides is like a fire that has to be fed continually—more and more is needed to fuel the fire. And it becomes a consuming fire that destroys human relationships. Porn will always fail us; all become victims to this sleek, appealing, dragon, beckoning users with its promise to fulfill all sexual desires, never giving implication to the death it will bring.

"Culturally and personally, I don't think we can afford to be casual about this topic any longer. It's literally changing brain pathways and demands more and more usage to get the same high. The reward center of our brain fires up when we accomplish a goal. The brain chemical dopamine is released, giving us the thrill that goes with accomplishment. Dopamine is secreted at moments of sexual excitement and novelty.

"Porn scenes filled with novel sexual acts fire the reward center. The ventral tegmental area (VTA) is the origin of the dopamine system and is the natural reward circuitry of the brain—it is a personal drug dispenser. The VTA looks for novelty and gives a big hit of dopamine when someone finds it. To get the same hit of dopamine, one has to seek new and novel images. The images are reinforced by the dopamine hit, altering the user's sexual tastes. What may have started as a way to learn about sex or spice things up with a sexual partner, ends up changing the sexual tastes of the user. This usage then damages the dopamine reward system, thus damaging the brain.

"Getting sex without the work of being in a relationship with a real person alters the reward center, so human beings lose their God-given motivation to pursue and court a spouse or person to be in relationship with. God intended oxytocin (the love hormone) to be released during lovemaking, which bonds and attaches a couple to one another. This sexual bonding, then helps couples have more grace for some of the annoying things that take place between two people.

"Solo sex does not provide this oxytocin release, thus, leaving its users more lonely and disconnected. I have lots of compassion for those who are sexually addicted to porn, because typically there are deeper hurts and wounds that need to be addressed. But I think it is vital we see it for the poison it is, even if all we recognize is how porn is not helping to create a more humane, empathic, and connected world. Instead, it is doing the opposite.

"I know many addicts did not receive sufficient bonding from their parents or most significant caregiver. God wanted every child to receive secure attachment, which means the child knew his or her parents would be available, warm, and nurturing, not perfect, but would work to build trust with the child. Dr. Daniel Siegel says it like this, 'Being a *we* often begins in our infancy. Yet, over one third of us have had a history of insecure attachment and did not have a reliable experience of joining in where we were respected as individuals who were worthy of being a part of a linked and vibrant whole.'[3]

"For children who did not get that type of attachment, they typically develop one of two styles of attachment: anxious or avoidant. The anxious attacher feels insecure and afraid when attachment isn't going well and typically ramps up emotionally to try to reconnect. The avoidant tamps down emotionally and moves away from attachment, believing he or she cannot trust attachment.

"The brain develops from the bottom to the top (our primal brain resides at the bottom and our pre-frontal cortex, our smart brain, resides at the top), and from right to left. The right side is the relational side of your brain, the left is the logical; and the left side was intended to help make sense of the right side. If the child, whose main task is to experience joyful, trusting connections with mother and father during its first eighteen months of life, did not receive these positive feelings to minimize and regulate stressful feelings, the child becomes the adult who has poor affect regulation. In other words, these adults have a hard time or an inability to calm and soothe themselves when stressed or to reach out to another human being for containment.

"You can understand how this person reaches for some sort of substance to calm the brain. God's ideal was we would reach for mommy or daddy to comfort, smile, reassure, and soothe our discomforts; but when that doesn't happen the child learns people cannot be trusted, and they must find ways on their own to soothe the distress.

"Because caregivers didn't provide what was needed for this child, shame gets deeply wired into the limbic system, where memories are stored. Shame is generally programmed by the time we are two years old. This is why we oftentimes don't have the language to describe our shame; we just have feelings of shame.

"On a side note, research reveals the best predictor of a child's attachment is actually how a parent has made sense of his or her own early life history. Even foster or adoptive parents with a coherent narrative revealing how they've made sense of their life histories help their non-genetically related children develop secure relationships with them.[4] When we process our traumas, big or small, it rewires our brains, brings healing to our narratives, and frees us to walk in the abundant life Jesus longs for us to live.

"Shame says there is something inherently wrong with me: I am less than others, or I am more than others. Shame's greatest lie is, 'You are unworthy of relational connection.' Shame is at the root of all relationship disturbances and is the great kidnapper of intimacy. Shame sends us into hiding and isolation and deeper into attachment and intimacy disorders. Further, shame invites people into one-night stands, casual sex, unattached sex, lust, and porn.

"The reason this type of sex is so appealing is because it doesn't require letting another person in. But God's idea of healthy sexuality is based in a context of relationship with another person free from shame, a relationship where you are allowing yourself to be known and you are longing to know the other.

"Neuroscientists say our brains are not fully developed until we are twenty-five. That means we needed sexual and relational guidance, teaching, and wisdom until we were twenty-five and ready to make good sexual and relational choices. How many of you wish you would have had more guidance?"

Most in the room nodded.

Olivia, wanting to be sensitive to give the group time to process said, "I know we have covered a lot of information this session. Let's get into our groups and process for a few minutes and then we will take a lunch break.

"I'll put some questions on the screen. Take about forty-five minutes to process with your group. Make it safe for each other and avoid giving advice. Mostly, what we want to do is listen. Psalms 10:17–18 says, 'The victim's faint pulse picks up; the hearts of the hopeless pump red blood as you put your ear to their lips. Orphans get parents, the homeless get homes. The reign of terror is over, the rule of the gang lords is ended.'

"Some of you have felt terrorized and ruled over by sexual issues, you have felt like orphans and even like you didn't have a place to belong. Today, let's be the kind of people who just put our ear to the lips of the victims with kindness and compassion. Let's give a home for one another's narratives; and let's love, like a good parent loves a child."

MOVING FORWARD

1. What value did your family put on human sexuality and sex education?
2. Who talked with you about your sexual values and what did they say?
3. What feelings did you have when we talked about the impact porn has on the brain? Do you feel more empathy for those who struggle?

4. What would you like your takeaway from this event to be? What are you hoping for?

PART II: AFTERNOON SESSION

After everyone returned from lunch and settled into their chairs, Olivia started the session by asking a question.

"How do people heal from sexual mistakes, porn addiction, abuse, boredom, and dislike of sex? What needs to happen to become whole?"

The room was still, as minds were searching for answers to the questions.

Kaycie raised her hand and offered, "Well, for me, it has included moving out of my denial, not blaming James for everything, and facing my own sexual brokenness by telling others my story. It has also included being in a safe group with other people who won't judge me, or condemn me, or give me advice, but instead they listen, care, and show me they understand. It has required me to trust that God wants to heal me, and He is for me.

"For a long time, I was really mad at God and I blamed Him for what happened to me. But I'm grateful God was okay with me yelling at Him and getting my anger up and out; once I did that, I realized He was most likely as mad as I was that bad things happened to me sexually. Once I understood He cares and hurts with me, I let Him in and asked Him to heal me. He has and is. He led me to the group I am in, He led me here today, and He gave me a husband who is working on his own healing process. I have accepted this is a journey and my issues will not magically go away or get better on their own. I have to actively engage in the process, but, if I do, the process will work.

"I already see a difference in myself. The shameful, critical judge in my head is getting quieter. I am feeling more confident, something I lost after I was sexually assaulted. And I'm reclaiming parts of myself I didn't even realize were stolen or given away. I like myself more and the self-hatred has diminished."

"Kaycie, thank you for sharing with us what has worked for you." Olivia smiled.

"Does anyone else want to share their experience?"

Evan, Emily's husband, spoke up, "Well, my story is a little different. Emily had to force me to get help. I was about to lose everything—my wife, my kids, my future—if I didn't do something. She reached her limit of my emotional distance and checked my internet history to see what I was looking at. I blamed her for our sexual problems, when, truth be told, I was the one avoiding her, because I felt guilty for what I was doing behind her back. It wasn't until I went and saw a therapist that I started to unpack my story. It's still hard to talk about."

"Do you want to tell us more?" Olivia invited.

"Yeah, it's good practice, and what I have noticed is the more I tell it, the less shame I feel about it. So, I had an older cousin and he introduced me to porn and then wanted me to do some of the stuff to him we saw. It was exciting, but also revolting, so sex got really confusing for me. This went on for three years. Even with Emily, I wanted her, but I also felt anxious about getting that close to her.

"After what happened with my cousin, I just started to shut down and not let people get too close to me. Porn felt okay, because it met my need for sex without letting another human in. Since I started seeing a therapist, I have worked through the sexual abuse with my cousin and I am working on learning how to let Em in. It is a journey and I hope she will stay with me long enough for us to see if we can form a secure attachment to each other. I don't blame her for being angry with me. She has put up with a lot." You could see Emily soften as she reached over and took Evan's hand.

"Emily, what are you experiencing right now?" Olivia wondered.

"Hearing Evan's story gives me empathy for him—something I had lost. I feel closer to him, because he is letting me in and telling me his story," she said.

Evan replied, "Yeah, it's the weirdest thing. I thought if she knew the real me she would run like crazy to get away from me. Instead, telling her my story has created a bond we have never experienced."

"Is anybody identifying with Evan and Emily?" Yeses could be heard and people could be seen in the room connecting to their story.

"Isn't it true, emotional vulnerability builds an emotional connection? Telling our stories helps connect us to ourselves, God, and others, and it builds shame resiliency. In other words, shame loses much of its power when we share our experiences."

HEALING IN PROCESS

"I want to spend the rest of this session talking about how we heal. Let's start by talking about the idea of integration.

Integration is at the heart of well-being. Dr. Daniel Siegel says it like this, 'Integration, which entails the linkage of different aspects of a system—whether they exist within a single person or a collection of individuals—is seen as the essential mechanism of health as it promotes a flexible and adaptive way of being that is filled with vitality and creativity. The ultimate outcome of integration is harmony. The absence of integration leads to chaos and rigidity.'[5]

"In other words, he is saying our brains need to be brought into harmony with the different parts of itself. The brain is made of different parts, and, sometimes, because of the way we were raised, we tend to keep the parts separate. Mind science is teaching us the integrated brain is the happy brain. Dr. Siegel is also saying we need each other. Our brains are happier with other brains, than they are isolated and separate.

"Community with others helps regulate our brains, bringing order to chaos, connection where there has been disconnection, and consistency where there was inconsistency. The confused self becomes settled and focused when in community. As the song title says, *Loneliness is Such a Sad Affair.*[6]

"He also states, 'Making sense of our history integrates the brain.'[7] People help us make sense of our history through listening, validation, feedback, and showing compassion for our story. From the beginning of time, God has invited all of us into this integrated harmony. That is why He asked Adam and Eve a question—it's not that He needed an answer—He was asking for their benefit. He was engaging their brains (the emotional brain with the linear brain, the relational brain with the logical brain).

"Psalm 11:7 says this, 'God's business in putting things right; He loves getting the lines straight, setting us straight.' God's desire is to help us integrate the narrative of our lives. No matter how our history developed, He is interested in inspiring us to rewire. He, more than anyone, knows how rewirable our brains are. It's never too late.

"So how do you do this rewiring process?

1. "We put ourselves in loving, compassionate, kind, and trusting environments.

"Please remember, if you were wired to not trust, this will be a challenge for you. You will look for ways people are failing you. You will be hyper alert in finding the smallest infraction in how a person or people have disappointed you. Please, please, please, get and stay connected to *good enough* people. There are no perfect people; we disappoint each other. Unless people are evil or foolish, stay connected. Admit you have a hard time trusting, and then work on your trust issues. But have grace for yourself. And admit that trusting people is scary for you. Have a few select people you can ask for a reality check.

"For example, if someone didn't call you back as fast as you wanted, ask your reality check person if that is a good reason to write that person off. Instead of getting all fired up about a perceived infraction, stop, tune in to yourself, tune in to what your reality test person is saying, calm yourself, and stay connected. People will disappoint you, but that doesn't make him or her a bad person. It may just mean they had something going on, like the flu, or a sick kid, or a cranky boss. Develop your ability to be patient.

2. "Tell your story over and over until your history begins to make sense to you.

"If you are more avoidant in your attachment style, you may find yourself saying, 'I don't remember anything about my childhood.' Or if you had dismissive parents, you may have learned how to dismiss your own narrative and emotions. If you had a parent who flooded you with his or her problems or emotions, you may feel flooded by your own emotions. So ask others to help you develop emotional regulation.

"Also, hearing other people's stories may overwhelm you. If this happens to you, picture yourself in your own *hula hoop*, separate from the person telling their story. You don't have to carry anyone else's story, you are in community to care, but not to carry. Remember, we are attempting to heal your brain and bring harmony to your life. So, start exploring what you do remember. Don't dismiss your story as insignificant. Keep pressing in validating to yourself and others, 'We heal by telling.' Ask God to help you remember, He longs to heal your life as much as you want your life healed.

3. "Attune, tune in, be present. Many children who didn't receive a secure attachment learned how to fragment. We frequently call it compartmentalizing. It sounds like such a good idea and it is when we are focused on accomplishing a task. But when it comes to our lives, the well-being of our souls, we need to tune in to what we are feeling, experiencing, and needing.

"Start asking yourself questions such as: *What am I feeling right now?* Then wait until you have a name for the emotion. Ask yourself, *What do I see, hear, smell, taste? What do I experience when I touch something or someone? What is my body saying to me? Am I hungry, tired? Do I need to breathe deep, stretch, go for a walk, calm my brain by looking at the sky?*

"We are learning by doing and practicing. So let's take a break and get back into our groups. We are going to process how to be a loving, compassionate, and kind community to one another. Let's talk about our trust issues and how trust was shaped and formed in our lives, and then let's tune in to what we are experiencing. Notice when your breathing changes, name your emotions, and ask for what you need. The questions for this group time are on the screen. Listen and learn from each other. But before you break, let me pray for you.

"Jesus, You are the healer of our lives, our hearts, brains, and emotions. We invite You into the process time and pray You would help us connect the data with our emotions. Help us connect the right side of our beautiful brain with the left. You are a good Father who longs to gather up His children and hold them near, as You rewire our broken places. Amen."

MOVING FORWARD

1. What was growing up like in your family?
2. How did your parents build trust with you?
3. Give three words describing your relationship with your mom, three for your dad. Share the descriptions with your group. For example: Mom was warm and present, or maybe cold and angry. Dad was fun and kind, or violent and critical.
4. How was that for you to share part of your story with the group?
5. Locate and name an emotion you are experiencing right now. Example: scared, sad, angry, disgusted,

annoyed, frustrated, lost, or compassion, wonder, hope, empathy...

6. Invite the presence of Jesus into these memories and into your story.

TEN

Cultivating Happiness

"There are three elements we want to cultivate to create healthy relationships and healthy sexual relating. What are these three elements? They are: intimacy, attachment, and passion.

1. *"Intimacy*—learning to be intimate with another person means we practice opening up and letting them in. It means we are willing to tolerate the risk of being known and knowing the other. It means we practice vulnerability and honesty, which builds trust in the relationship. We can accept and grieve the negative realities of loving another person. We understand we are not with a perfect person. They have strengths and weaknesses; they have flaws and areas in need of growth—just like we do.

"As intimacy grows, so does security. A relationship cannot move to attachment without intimacy, which is the capacity to let another person see and know you, and to have the relational intelligence to want to know the other. If I won't let you in to know me, you have nothing to attach to, and if you won't let me in, I can't attach to you.

2. "*Attachment*—Attachment is when we allow ourselves to connect deeply to another person. Anxiety and avoidance are acknowledged and overcome by practicing vulnerability and openness about fears. Help is asked for and sought, when one or both partners find themselves stuck in negative relational patterns. Each take personal responsibility to do his or her own growth work. They avoid the blame game and instead ask themselves the question, *What is my part in this?* Attachment takes time to build and includes commitment and covenant. To form a secure, solid attachment, people want to know three things: 1) Do you have my back? 2) Can I count on you? 3) Are you there for me? When those three questions are answered, secure attachment can form. Secure attachment makes possible true, lasting, sexual passion.

3. "*Passion*—To build passion, fear of closeness is acknowledged and processed, and both spouses are willing to be naked and unashamed, because trust has been built. This couple has built a solid friendship which includes empathic caring, listening, and emotional closeness. They have figured out how to be connected but separate. They do not avoid or cling, but celebrate differences and self-differentiation, which develops through secure attachment. Because of this, they have the potential to become lovers—where they share their bodies, welcome sexual arousal, desire, curiosity, and play.

"Together and separately, they have worked on becoming well-defined, mature lovers, able to communicate likes and pleasurable feelings, make requests, and ask for what is desired sexually. Passion is allowed to ebb and flow and develop over time. False sexual expectations are worked through and bridges are built to overcome sexual dysfunctions and difficulties. Grace for the humanity of the other is extended and practiced, so passion has fertile soil in which to grow.

"We realize that anything beautiful takes time to build. Intimacy, attachment, and passion, are not grown overnight or casually, but take deliberate pursuit. It's true that anything worth creating takes time, effort, and diligence.

"How do we get to intimacy, attachment, and passion? Let's unpack the term *intimacy*. Genesis 4:1 says, "Adam knew his wife Eve." Adam *yada* Eve, a Greek term meaning to perceive, to know intimately, to understand, to experience. It means Adam sexually knew, experienced, and understood his wife Eve.

"Genesis 18:19 says, 'God said, For I have known (chosen) him' (Amplified Bible Translation). God is saying He knew Abraham personally and intimately. *Yada* also speaks of man knowing God. Moses asked the Lord to teach him His ways so he may know Him; to know Him is to have an experiential knowledge of Him. Paul said in Philippians 3:10, 'I desire to know Him and the power of His resurrection.' Paul desired to intimately know God.

"This term signifies an intimate, experiential, personal, face to face, eye to eye, I to I, type of a relationship. It isn't casual and it isn't quick. This type of relationship takes the willingness to study and observe and watch and listen and attune to and notice. Honestly, it takes work, but it is the kind of work that is more like an investment. The more you invest, the greater the reward.

"How would lovemaking be different if you approached it with this term in mind? If this is what you were made for?"

The room was still for a few moments while Olivia patiently waited.

James motioned with his raised hand he wanted to say something. "Well, it gives sex a totally different meaning. If I initiate sex with Kaycie from a position of wanting to know her—I want to understand her. I want to experience her—I imagine I would be thinking less about having an orgasm with her and more about really being with her, being present with her. I would have to bring *myself* fully to bed. I couldn't be hidden, or preoccupied. I would have her as my focus and my heart in the right place.

"If I want to know her, I would be focused on discovering what pleases her sexually and how I could engage her whole person. I would see her not just as a body, but a person with a soul, spirit, and personality. I would care about her needs, her desires, her likes and dislikes. I would listen for what arouses her. I would notice when she goes quiet or when it feels like she has left the room mentally. I would ask her where she went. I would ask her what she feels and likes and wants. I would be way more sensitive to her."

With that, he sat back down with tears filling his eyes. Olivia asked him, "James, what might you be feeling?"

James closed his eyes for a minute before he said, "I haven't ever really made love to my wife. It just hit me; I haven't known how to make love to her. I thought it was all about getting it on with her because I wanted her, but now I know it's deeper than that. I want to *know* her."

He turned and looked at Kaycie, "Would you forgive me for not getting it? Would you forgive me for being selfish?"

"I forgive you, James; I haven't known how to make love to you any more than you have known how to make love to me. I totally forgive you. Will you forgive me for withholding and withdrawing from you?" Kaycie asked.

"Of course, I will. Man, I don't deserve you." James smiled. They leaned into each other for a tender kiss.

Olivia asked, "How is that for you two?"

Kaycie offered, "My heart feels warm, like there is something resonating deeply inside me. I know it's right and true and how God wants lovemaking to be for us."

James agreed. "Same for me. I feel a little sad it has taken me this long to get it, but I also am happy I am getting it! Can we go home early and practice this new knowing?"

Everyone laughed, including Kaycie, who shook her head and rolled her eyes.

Olivia added, "Let's take a few minutes for you to process with your spouse how lovemaking would be different if the focus was on intimate knowing. If you are here without a spouse, process with another person how this idea challenges your views of sex."

Olivia gave the group time to process with each other.

"How was that for you? Would someone like to share with the group?"

Joe, Holly's husband, raised his hand. "Some of you know a little bit about our history. Holly and I are fairly new Christians, and, honestly, our sexuality was really shaped by the views of what the world says is good. We were into all kinds of stuff. And this is a totally different perspective, but, like James and Kaycie said, it feels right. Holly and I want this; we want to learn how to make love like this. Honestly, the stuff we were into left us both feeling lonely. We had lots of kinky sex, but it didn't connect us. We had some great orgasms and plenty of lust, but something was always missing, and we knew it. This way of making love feels like it engages the heart, and I guess that would be what makes all the difference."

"Thanks, Joe. That's insightful," Olivia acknowledged. "You make a great point. In God's kingdom, doesn't everything come down to the condition of our hearts? Doesn't every big issue we face have something to do with what is going on inside us? Is our *flesh* ruling our lives, or have we surrendered our desires to His desires?

"I'm thinking that when we understand God created eroticism and He actually loves it when a husband and wife make love passionately, it delights Him. Then we can trust Him and surrender our way of having sex to His way of making love. If there is one thing I have learned, after many decades of loving and being a follower of Jesus, it is His ways are always so much better than my ways.

"So let's transition into talking about attachment for a few minutes. Why is attachment a big deal when it comes to making love?" Olivia asked the group.

Angie responded, "You know my history, and how I have been terrified to let myself attach to my husband—I was so afraid of being known I had an affair to try to destroy what little attachment we did have." She looked at her husband to see if she was saying too much. He gave her the nod to go ahead. "I can't believe he has decided to stay with me. His not leaving me has made me believe in attachment. I feel wanted by him.

"I have never felt wanted. I think I had the affair to see if he would pursue me or dump me because I was too much trouble. I felt that way with my mom, like I was just too much trouble. I figured Dylan would prove me right, but I'm grateful he proved me wrong. I'm feeling things for him like I have never felt for anyone and I think it's because his actions are saying to me, 'I am attached to you even when you hurt me. You can't run me off that easily.' Wow, that's love. You remember how I wanted to get rid of him. Now I can't get enough of him! This attachment thing is actually really sexy."

Olivia smiled, while her eyes filled with tears. *Yes*, she thought to herself, *they are getting it.*

"Angie, you said that so well. Dylan, thanks for coming today. You are our hero. It took guts to stay. I think your faithfulness has won your wife's heart. We know that wasn't easy. It took courage to stay," Olivia celebrated.

"Angie, you said it, attachment is sexy. When we are securely attached to our mate, it releases all kinds of feel-good hormones, security, and safety. It provides a couple a safe haven from the ravages of the world. When you have earned secure attachment, you know, whatever happens, you have someone by your side, someone who has your back, and someone to come home to at the end of a day. As a culture, we have been so dismissive about how beautifully sexy attachment is. A solid, secure attachment lays a foundation for some erotic passion."

Evan, in the back of the room said, "How? How does attachment build erotic passion? I don't get it."

Olivia nodded, "We have made detachment so sexy. Think about all of the James Bond movies. He is the quintessential sexy male. He has hot sex with women, but never allows himself to give his heart—he purposely stays disconnected. Think how detached, handsome, movie star men have groomed all of us to decide what is sexy and what isn't. The one time James Bond gave his heart to a woman was the one time he married, but she was tragically murdered as they drove off to celebrate their new life together. The message was clear—men, don't give your hearts— it will only end in tragedy. Keep that heart of yours tucked safely in the depths of your belly. Don't let her think you are getting attached because then she will hurt you.

"Women, how many movies have we watched where a man breaks a woman's heart? He leaves her or betrays her and she decides the only way to protect her heart from being hurt again is to harden her heart. We have all been trained by this world's messages that attachment is dangerous. When Dr. John Bowlby started to uncover the need for secure attachment in children and reported those findings to his colleagues, his colleagues nearly tarred and feathered him. I think we have allowed detached people to teach us about relationships, instead of letting the attached Father God, who is completely and wholly in love with His children, be our teacher. He is our relationship model. In order to learn from Him we have to examine the condition of our hearts, which oftentimes have been torn in pieces.

"Maybe it's time we bring our sexuality and the heart by which we have been operating to the Father. We don't have much to bring in this area of our lives except for brokenness. He is the redeemer of all things and loves to mold, shape, redo, lead, teach, and create something so beautiful from what's broken. It's what He does. We can never forget He is the God of the impossible, the improbable, and the highly unlikely. What if He could and would most happily take the messes of your sexuality, the broken, and make it beautiful? Would you let Him? Would you surrender this significant part of your life that has caused you significant pain to the King?"

There was a reverent hush, as each person examined his or her heart and pondered the question. *Will I let Him in, or will my shame and need to do things my way rule in this moment? My heart has been torn in pieces, but will I trust God to take the broken parts and make me whole? Or will I proudly hold onto my way?* The questions hung in the air—waiting for answers.

"All of us come to crossroads in our lives, hopefully many. Crossroads are a point in time when we need to stop and pay attention. We need to look to the right and to the left and determine what our next course of action will be. Will I doggedly stick to my belief system and do it the way I always have because it is what I know? Or will I open my heart and allow change to take place?"

Evan said, "Olivia, I have tried it my way for so long, and my life is a mess. My sexuality has done nothing but hurt me and those I love. I have cheated, lied, deceived, manipulated, and blamed. I have nearly destroyed what I have with Emily. She had every right to walk away from me and take our children with her. Do you think God would have me? Do you think He would want someone like me? Do you think he would want a cheater and a liar and someone who is hooked on porn?"

"Evan, I think you are exactly who Jesus wants. I think He has been seeking you out and calling your name. I think He has loved you since before you were in your mother's womb. Evan, you are the one He gave up the life of his Son Jesus for. You are wanted by the Father. He wants to adopt you, put His royal robe on your shoulders, and His ring on your finger. He wants to call you His son and his friend. He wants to heal the sexual mistakes you have made, and He wants to cast your sin and shame as far as the east is from the west. You are the one He wants," Olivia reassured.

Evan sat with his eyes closed and tears streaming down onto his chest. Emily held his hand and cried with him. She thought to herself, *God, you are the God of miracles. And I am experiencing a miracle in this moment. Thank you. Thank you.*

"This feels like a hallowed moment. Is anyone else experiencing God's presence?" Olivia asked.

Olivia had noticed a man, who looked like he was in his late twenties, slip into the room at the beginning of the session. He now stood to his feet at the back of the room.

Olivia said, "Yes, is there something you would like to say?"

He cleared his throat and shuffled his feet for a moment before he spoke.

"Hi, everyone, I hope you don't mind. I came in late. I'm Vanessa's husband, Justin." He gave Vanessa a sheepish wave with the palm of his hand and then looked back down at his feet. "I left Vanessa six months ago. It's not that I wanted to. It ripped my guts out. I just didn't think I had a choice. She shut me out, pushed me away with her silence, and we never had sex. I couldn't take it anymore, so I told her she had to get help for whatever was eating her alive.

"I hadn't heard a word from her for six months, and then I got a text from her the other day telling me she joined a women's group and finally told her story. I don't even know her story. She

wondered if I wanted to come today. I didn't answer her text…"
he said, looking up at Vanessa, "because I didn't know what to
say. But today is the first day I have felt hope in months that
maybe, just maybe, if we both let God in, our marriage might
have a chance. What do you think, Vanessa? Do we have a
chance? Do you want me back? Do you have any love for me
left?" With that Justin shoved his hands deep into the recesses
of his jean pockets.

Every eye turned to the front of the room where Vanessa sat.
She seemed frozen.

"Vanessa," Olivia prompted as she went and stood beside
her, "would you like to respond to Justin?"

Vanessa slowly got up from her chair and walked to the back
of the room where Justin stood. She stood in front of him with
her eyes locked on his. After what seemed like an eternity, she
put her arms around his neck and put her head on his chest.
Finally, she pleaded, "Please come home."

As silly as it sounds, the room erupted in cheers. Suddenly,
Justin moved out of her embrace, everyone paused—*maybe the
rejection had been too much and he couldn't risk letting her
in*—when a warm smile broke across his face.

He said, "I would love to, with one condition."

"Yes, what is it?" Vanessa asked.

"You stay in your women's group, and we get connected with
this group of people. We can't do it alone. We both know that
didn't work, and it most likely never will. We are going to need
all the help we can get to make it." Vanessa nodded in agreement.

Olivia stood in the front of the room and shook her head,
looking for the words to say. "I'm so moved and deeply humbled

by your vulnerable sharing. You have all touched my heart in many different ways. And I'm honored to watch as God's word comes to life. He does take what the enemy meant for evil and uses it for our good. Only God can do that. Thank you for being real today, for being open and vulnerable, for contending for your marriages, and for your own souls. How about I pray for you and then we will have some group time?" Olivia offered.

"Father, I am grateful for this group of people. Their vulnerability has melted my heart and reminded me of why we are better together. You are the one who said to never forsake getting together. We are all humbled by your presence and how we have felt you interacting with us on this topic. I get the impression you are overjoyed we are talking about what is so dear to Your heart."

MOVING FORWARD

Here are questions to ponder:

1. Have you been making love or having sex?
2. How are you "knowing" your spouse? Or what are you doing to cultivate *yada*?
3. How is your attachment? Are you avoidant? What happened in your childhood to cause you to become avoidant?
4. How can you practice letting your spouse in?
5. If you were to share something no one knows about you, what would it be?

ELEVEN

Hold Me

What's a self-fulfilling prophecy? Well, let me give you an example. Growing up, I wanted my dad's love and attention. So I tried all kinds of ways to get it, and, at times, I felt loved by him. Then other times, he would flip a switch and become violent and raging. He was terrifying in those moments, and I believed if he truly loved me he wouldn't be violent toward me and hurt me.

Sadly, I have carried that belief into my own marriage. I can feel completely loved by Ron, until occasionally something happens to trigger that pain inside me. As quickly as I can bat my eyelashes, I can sink into that old belief that the most significant man in my life doesn't love me. I start to rehearse the same verse from childhood. *If Ron really loved me he would...* fill in the blank.

Then, I start looking for evidence he doesn't love me, so my brain can say, *See, I told you so.* It's not based on reality. Ron loves me and cognitively I know that 100 percent, all of the time. Ron isn't my dad. He isn't violent. He is a good man to be married to—the best. But my primal brain remembers the fear it felt when my dad went ballistic and how that self-fulfilling prophecy got wired into my system. It's a painful place and I have had to grieve the losses of love I felt in my childhood and continue to be aware when it is triggered. It rarely happens anymore. But if I am tired or overworked, I can fall into this pit and find myself rehearsing the ways I am not loved.

A self-fulfilling prophecy can be a positive or a negative expectation about circumstances, events, or people that can affect a person's behavior toward them in a manner causing those expectations to be fulfilled. Sometimes our belief system can play a part of our relational challenges. We all have a powerful need to prove our belief system is true—even if it is destructive to love and life.

THE REVELATION

Kaycie could feel the butterflies in her stomach doing flips—it felt like a fleet invaded her body. James announced last week at Real Life that Kaycie would be sharing her story, but she had been too busy chasing kids, wiping noses, and kissing boo-boos to think much about it. Now the day was here and she regretted agreeing to talk in front of five hundred college kids. She was afraid she would freeze or go blank—*then what*? she wondered. *What if I make a fool of myself*?

The back door closing shook her back into reality. Looking up, she saw the smiling face of James.

"Hey, you look lost in your thoughts," James said.

"Yeah, I'm sort of freaking out about tonight."

"I get that. Do you want to talk about it?"

"Well, I know I have done this for the last three years, but I'm not sure how it will go tonight. What if I blow it? What if I embarrass you? The ministry? What if they hate it and never come back?"

James held open his arms and said, "Come here." He scooped her up and held her close to his chest.

"Breathe. Let the fear go. You can't embarrass me. I have watched the students in the last three years and how they respond to you. Kaycie, they love you. And your story—well, you know how impactful it has been."

She felt her body relax as he held her, his body had a way of doing that these days. He melted her.

Later that day, after the boys were settled at her mom's and the house was quiet, Kaycie walked into her closet and picked out her sapphire blue heels—the ones Sam called her "rocket shoes." She wasn't sure why he called them that, but assumed it meant they were pretty great. He loved rockets. Perfect, she thought, a great pair of heels always makes everything better. She finished her outfit with a pair of skinny jeans and a pretty, sleeveless top that showed off her toned arms adorned with a touch of the "rocket blue."

As she put the finishing touches on her makeup, she whispered, "Jesus, help me, calm me, and tell our story through me. You are my healer and deliverer; may this bring You glory and draw the students closer to You and Your love."

James held her hand as they walked into the auditorium. Before she knew it, the announcements were made, the worship was over, and James was standing on the platform introducing her.

As she walked up to the platform, she could read the love in his eyes, and she knew that no matter how this went, his love was integrated into her soul in ways she hadn't realized. His love filled her with confidence. With James by her side and God's Spirit indwelling in her, she was suddenly ready to be in this moment. She paused before she spoke to take in the faces of these students she loved and the new faces she would love soon enough. Especially if she let them know her, the real, vulnerable, wounded, and healed parts of herself.

With a deep breath, she opened her mouth and allowed the story to flow out of her.

The students sat mesmerized. No one moved; you could have heard a pin drop. Eyes glistened with tears. One young man wrapped his arms around his girlfriend, signaling *I am here. Whatever happened to you, I want to be a safe man for you—I won't hurt you.*

Kaycie told the students how she trusted a man, a minister, who betrayed her. She didn't sugarcoat the rape and how it impacted her for several years until she got the help she needed. She shared how she loved James, but until the truth was uncovered and her soul healed, she couldn't really let him in. The youth pastor shattered her ability to trust. And it wasn't just the youth pastor; her own father was frequently abusive, so trusting a man was more than her heart would allow.

While speaking, it crossed her mind that perhaps she had needed James to cheat, to prove her belief system was true, *You can't trust a man; they all cheat.* Olivia talked with her about self-fulfilling prophecies, and how they can be a positive or a negative belief system that causes those expectations to be fulfilled.

For a split second, she recalled the brief conversation when Olivia asked her if her belief system played a part in the troubles she and James experienced. Olivia was clear that James's behavior was James's responsibility, but she also said we all have a powerful need to prove our belief system is true—even if it is destructive to love and life.

At that moment, while speaking to these students, Kaycie had her own epiphany. She could feel it and it was real; deep down she believed trusting a man was emotional suicide. Momentarily stunned by this revelation, she knew she had to make things right with James. So much progress had been made between the two of them, but there was more work to be done if they were ever going to be truly naked and unashamed with each other.

Wrapping up her talk, Kaycie asked the students if any of them experienced anything along the same lines as she did. She asked the student leaders and the Real Life team to come up to the front to be available to any of the students who needed support or prayer. It began slowly, but soon a throng of students flooded the front of the auditorium. Prayers, whispered truths, secrets were shared in this sacred space. Kaycie shook her head, always surprised by how many could relate to her story. It caused her to notice the heaviness in her heart, but just as quickly, the promise available for every student if they simply took hold of it. Jesus significantly healed her heart and was still doing so. And Jesus could heal their hearts too.

It was quiet in the car on the drive home. Both were processing the time with the students and hearing some of their stories of sexual trauma and regrets. Both felt contented to have the opportunity to do as Scripture recommends—*just put your ear to the lips of the victim and healing will begin.*

James interpreted her thoughts with, "You okay?"

"Yes, I'm just processing what all happened tonight and a realization I had about myself. I know you are tired, but can we have some talk time when we get home, maybe after we have a shower and unwind?"

"Sure, of course," James responded. "Hey, let's pray together before we get home so we can focus on each other."

"Father," he said aloud while he drove the car, "thanks for my wife who was willing to put it all out there tonight. Thanks that the students responded. We pray for each one of them, those who responded, and those who didn't. We ask You to wrap them up in Your arms of love and heal their messed-up lives. Thanks that You are the healer and we just get to participate in this adventure You have called us to. We trust You to do a good work in each of their lives and to keep working in ours. We love You, clearly because You first loved us God."

Kaycie threw her purse on the counter and headed to take a shower. She stood there for a long time, just letting the hot water run over her shoulders. Eventually, James poked his head into the shower and asked if he could join her. She smiled and said, "Sure, you can, but just FYI, I need to talk before we do anything else."

"Oh yeah, totally...I get that," James replied. His body brushed up against her as she made room for him in the tiny shower. She felt a warmth flood her body that wasn't typical.

Instead of feeling uncomfortable, Kaycie looked him in the eyes and held his gaze. Yep, he was melting her and as much as she wanted to have him right then and there she stepped out of the shower and grabbed her towel. She slipped into a beautiful white silk robe she bought wondering if she would ever be able to embrace the sexy side of herself. Tonight she felt ready.

"It's beautiful outside. Do you want a drink and we can sit on the back porch for a while?"

"Yeah, absolutely," James said, as he toweled off his hair. He waited for her as she poured them both a drink and came out and sat close beside him. He reached over and played with the strands of her hair fallen from the pile on top of her head.

"You look beautiful; you take my breath away. You were amazing tonight, so confident, so powerful. You filled my heart so full I thought it was going to burst with gratitude that you are my wife."

She smiled at him with her mouth and eyes. "James, I realized something tonight. Something so powerful it felt like an epiphany. I think it will change us. You know how you have commented on how it feels like I hold back a part of myself from you? And you have mentioned how I just blow you off and say I don't know what you are talking about?"

He nodded.

"Well, I finally know why. I wasn't aware of it until tonight, but while I was speaking I realized I have held a belief close to my heart and I have guarded it like Fort Knox. I realized I don't trust men. It started with my dad, then the youth pastor added to it, and then when we went through the infidelity and the porn you added to it. But I realized that part of me needed you to do some of the things you did. It's what I believed men do. I believed it so deeply that unknowingly I may have played a part in our marital difficulties."

"Kaycie, no, I can't let you own my mistakes, not one drop of it."

"James, I understand, but for me to really heal I have to own the fact I have held that belief in my heart and even Scripture says, "As a man or *woman* believes so shall it be." I looked for ways to push you away. I wanted an excuse to not be intimate with you. I wanted you to leave me alone instead of sharing myself with you. I have withheld from you. And that's on me." Tears filled her eyes; truth felt hard but freeing. "James, I don't want to do that anymore. I want to give myself to you like it's our first time together. Would you make love to me?"

James cocked his head to the side as his eyes widened. "Um, yeah, I would be thrilled to." The tease of his smile warmed Kaycie's heart. She knew he was a changed man and no longer wanted the type of sex where his head was filled with images of other women and where he wasn't present but was using her body for a sexual release. She could feel the difference in him and had felt it for months. He was a changed man and she was a changed woman. The hell they went through, the trauma, had led them both to face the brokenness of their lives and now there was redemption. With this new truth, Kaycie stood up, reached for his hand, and led him to the bedroom.

The next morning Kaycie quietly wrapped her robe around her contented body and headed to the back porch for a moment by herself before James woke and the kids came home from her mother's house. She lifted her eyes to the vast Texas morning sky, slashed with emerging colors defining the day ahead.

"So God, this is what I have been missing all of these years? Wow, I had no idea this is what you had in mind for a husband and wife. Pure sexual joy—thank you for the work you have done to bring us to this place. Thank you for taking what the enemy planned to use to destroy us and using it for good."

"I give you glory for healing the trauma, and now giving us something I never dreamt of. I pray all married couples would have what we shared last night. Thank you Father for inventing sex—it is good—it is very good."

FINAL THOUGHTS

Kaycie has discovered the secret to great sex. It's not what *Cosmo* says it is. It isn't twelve ways to give him or her mind-blowing orgasms. No, it's deeper than that. Great sex is the fruit of doing the hard work, the soul work, that is required to truly become a healthy self. The more you open your heart and invite the healing process in, the more likely you are to become and embrace the sexual creature you are. Willingly opening your heart and mind to healing opens up new possibilities to play, explore, and have fun together sexually.

The more you do the work of healthy self-differentiation, the more connected you can become and the more connected you are to yourself, God, and your spouse, and the greater the potential for building erotic, sexual experiences together. Sex is ultimately about the condition of our hearts. If our hearts are closed down and shut off, that impacts how open we are to sharing our bodies with the one we chose to say "I do" to.

Here are a few questions for you to ponder:

1. On a scale of one to ten, with ten being very open and one being closed, how open are you to the healing process?
2. Like myself and Kaycie, do you have any self-fulfilling prophecies? Especially in relation to love and sex?
3. What do you need to move forward in becoming a healthy sexual self?
4. When is the last time you invited your partner to make love to you?
5. When is the last time you initiated sex, if you aren't typically the one to initiate?

TWELVE

Passion

Psychologist Paul Eastwick of the University of Texas at Austin says, "Passion is best defined as a combination of sexual connection and attachment longing."[1] I like his definition. Many experts believe passionate monogamy is impossible, boring, and dull. Passion is supposed to provide a high, much like a drug, and you can't stay intoxicated forever with the same person. Several evolutionary biologists say men in particular are programmed to spread their seed around, assuring the survival of the species. Most want us to believe romantic love cannot be sustained and once it has died, it is gone. Let it go, get over it, and move on.

Such nonsense has disrupted our ability to think straight on this topic. God made us for permanent, solid, and secure attachments. There will be disruptions; romantic love is a series of connections and disconnections. But instead of moving away from one another and believing romantic love is dead, we need to move in, heal the traumatic or hurtful breech, and repair our love through empathic listening, attunement to the needs of our spouse, and touch.

Sex is a beautiful way to bridge an attachment breach when you have missed an attachment *cue* from your spouse. The comfort and warmth of your partner's skin on your skin can soothe the pain of separation. Many times, if sex is about connection and expressing love, bodies can repair and make up faster than our brains can. Powerful feel-good hormones are released when a man and a woman go chest to chest, belly to belly, skin on skin. Caressing, kissing, and touching sensitive erogenous zones helps you get out of your head and into your body. Sometimes, a couple just needs to put their annoyances or frustrations on the shelf and make love to each other.

I'm not talking about putting a bandage on abuse; abuse is wrong—always. There is no excuse for emotional, physical, or verbal abuse. If abuse is going on in your relationship, stop everything, don't pass go, get help. Now! What I am talking about is the average marriage, where there is connection and disconnection, we hear each other and we misunderstand each other, we have moments of sensitivity and moments of insensitivity, we have days of attunement and times where we are un-attuned. Even great mothers miss attuning to their children's needs up to 70 percent of the time. When she realizes she missed her baby's cue, she responds and repairs.

We are going to miss each other as husband and wife on occasion, but it doesn't mean we should find excuses to neglect our sexual relationship. This part of a marital union is important. It has more value than we have assigned it. We can treat it casually and think it is supposed to happen like in the movies: automatic desire, instant arousal, spontaneous orgasm. That is silly. We have to work at anything worth having. Don't neglect this part of your relationship, even if it hasn't been great.

I think God thinks it is great when we make an effort to make love to our partner even if fireworks don't happen; there is still goodness happening. Just being together is good. Caressing, kissing, holding, cuddling, playing, and fondling are all good. We need to take the focus off of having intercourse and an orgasm and put the value on giving each other pleasure. Pleasure is underrated. Pleasure for your body and giving your spouse pleasure is worthy of our time and effort. God wants you to have the feel-good hormones released in your body to make marriage easier. It's like a free mini-vacation—why wouldn't you go?

So, what if my spouse doesn't like making love? Great question. There is a reason someone doesn't like sex. Instead of personalizing it and making it about yourself, why not explore with your spouse what they don't like. Be empathic, listen, ask good questions. Maybe she or he feels pressured. Maybe she feels misunderstood or taken for granted. Maybe he feels like he is supposed to be a sexual machine.

Men, especially after your wife has a baby, you have to tune into her more, not less. I know it's hard. Husbands can feel like they have been replaced with this little person who is having a love affair with your woman, or maybe your wife is having postpartum depression. It's not easy; be patient and sensitive. God has provided a beautiful opportunity to mature you into a sensitive partner to the woman He has given you.

Be present with her; ask her what she needs and how you can support her. Tell her you miss being sexually close with her and what that means to you, but reassure her you will wait until she is ready. Connect with her emotionally. It's really tempting after children come for the husband to just work more hours because he feels neglected. Move in toward her, not away.

Sexy takes on new meaning for a woman once she has children. Helping her with the kids is the sexiest thing you can do. I remember watching Ron playing with the boys and thinking, *Wow, that man is the sexiest thing on the earth and I can't wait to get him alone after those kids of ours go to bed!* I am telling you, woo her by helping her.

Women, I want to caution you, it's so easy to judge a man and think all he wants is sex; or the other extreme, he never wants me anymore. Get into your own solid self and pursue him sexually. Men want to be wanted as much as a woman wants to be wanted. No one wants to be judged for his or her sexual desires or lack of desire. If you don't want him pawing at you then give him reassurance that he is desirable by pursuing him. In the Song of Solomon it is the woman who opens the book by saying, "Kiss me—full on the mouth! Yes! For your love is better than wine, headier than your aromatic oils" (Song of Sol. 1:2). If you carefully read this book about marital sexual love and desire, you will find she frequently pursues him. She openly desires him. She asks for his affection. She regards him. She freely loves him pleasuring her body. She allows herself to soak in and receive sexual pleasure.

They say men love to make their women happy. Let him make you happy! This Song of Solomon woman says, "When my

King-Lover lay down beside me, my fragrance filled the room, His head resting between my breasts the head of my lover was a sachet of sweet myrrh, my beloved is a bouquet of wildflowers picked just for me from the fields of Engedi" (Song of Sol. 1:12–14). Maybe part of the problem we women have with finding, maintaining, and expressing sexual desire is because of the way we think and what we say to ourselves about our man. She calls him my King-Lover.

Okay, I get it, she is marrying the most powerful man in the world, but what man doesn't want to feel like he is the man you look up to, adore, and respect. What man doesn't want to be his wife's *lover*. She thinks so highly of him she is turned on just thinking about him—right? I mean she says, when he lies down beside her, her fragrance fills the room—she is saying, she is wet with arousal—*just saying*.

Remember the brain is the female's most important sex organ. Whatever you are saying to yourself about this man of yours will translate directly into how you feel sexually about him and yourself. When he lays his head between her breasts, she just breathes him in and recalls the beautiful love they make together. She isn't focusing on how he leaves his dirty clothes on the floor or the bodily noises he seems to enjoy making. No, she focuses on how he makes her body feel and the amazing things he does to her. It's a sensual feast. She engages her sense of smell and taste, and what she hears and sees, which ignites her sexually.

And men, this is one smart lover in that he talks to her. He tells her how beautiful she is. He says things like, "You remind me of Pharaoh's well-groomed and satiny mares. Pendant earrings line the elegance of your cheeks, strands of jewels illumine the curve of your throat. I'm making jewelry for you, gold and silver jewelry that will mark and accent your beauty" (Song of Sol. 1:9–11). This man pays attention; he notices.

Have you stood and admired a field of beautiful, satiny mares recently? If you haven't you should. The muscles, the intricate details of a well-groomed horse, are beyond beautiful—it's majestic. My dad raised thoroughbred race horses, and they have the most beautiful legs created.

I think Solomon was taking time to notice his woman. He even noticed her earrings and decided to make her more pairs to accent her beautiful cheeks. Guys, stop at Anthropologie and get the woman a pair of earrings. It goes a long way when she has been home all day wiping your darling children's bottoms and sweeping the cheerios off the floor for the fifth time in one day. Seriously, you absolutely cannot take her for granted and think she is going to want to make love to you. You have to make love to her heart first, and then she will happily open up and make love to your body.

Don't try to fix her. She doesn't want to be a problem you fix, she wants to be the woman you adore. She will glow with your love if you adore her. You adore her by paying attention, being sweet, helping her out, making her your priority. So many women tell me they desperately wanted their man when they were dating and then after getting married everything fizzled. The sizzle was gone. I think the reason this can happen is because men can be so goal oriented. When dating, she was the prize to win, so he paid attention, asked her out on dates, showered, and showed up smelling good and looking handsome.

After marriage some men can think, *I got my woman and now I can move on to my next conquest.* Good luck with that. No woman wants to be a conquest and then be basically hung on the wall like some kind of trophy because you have moved on to something more exciting. She wants to be the prize you won for the rest of your life.

If you treat her this way, she will most likely respond to you. If she doesn't respond, then my guess would be something happened in her history that has disrupted her God-given desire and arousal system. If that is your woman, go to her and tell her how much you love her and how much you care for her. If something bad happened to her, you want to be the one man in her life who will be by her side. You will walk through whatever it was that happened to her. You aren't going anywhere and you will be there, not to fix her, but to care for her. Ask her what she needs and ask her if she will open up; and tell her what that would mean to you.

Be vulnerable, for example: "I see you. I am thinking you have been hurt. I feel sad, and I want you to know I want you to enjoy sex. I want it to be great for you. What do you need, babe?" I know you men have been trained to think emotions are for girls, but every woman wants to be nurtured by her man. Think about it, we women nurture your children, probably buy the gifts for your mother's birthday, nurture you by feeding you and doing laundry, nurture the dog, tend the plant growing in the kitchen window, even nurture our friends and other people's children. But she needs you to nurture her. Nurture her with non-sexual touch. Hold her hand, put your arm around her, put your hand on the small of her back when you lead her into a room. Give her a foot rub while watching TV. They say the foot mimics our organs, so guess where her sexual organs might be located and zero in on that spot in a sweet and subtle way. Nurturing her most likely won't come naturally to you. Find an older man who gets it and ask him to teach you how to relate to and nurture your woman. It will be worth it, you will have a more contented and appreciative woman.

Another thing, Solomon treats his woman like a friend and invites her to come close to him. He says it like this, "Get up, my dear friend, fair and beautiful lover—come to me! Look around you: winter is over; the winter rains are over, gone! Spring flowers are in blossom all over. The whole world's a choir—and singing!…Oh, get up, dear friend, my fair and beautiful lover—come to me!" (Song of Sol. 2:13).

Can you picture this scene? This is what I envision—she is a little depressed, maybe she is hormonal and feeling blue, maybe they had a fight and she is feeling hopeless. He first calls her his friend—he is emotionally attuned to her—then he reminds her he thinks she is beautiful. Guys, every woman needs to hear that from her man. We get insecure about our looks and our bodies. About the time we accept our bodies, we have another baby, go through menopause, notice a new wrinkle, gain a few pounds, one of the kids gets sick and the gym becomes a distant memory, slip a disc and can't move—it's not easy. And we females need a little encouragement—you still find me attractive? What, this old body turns you on? You want me? Okay, she thinks, maybe there is hope, maybe we aren't over, maybe we can reconnect.

He does something else that really helps a woman. He tells her in his own words, "Babe, everything is going to be okay. Look, the flowers are blooming, the birds are singing, it's going to be okay. We are going to be okay." Women tend to catastrophize on occasion, even the healthiest of women. When you tell her, "We are going to make it. We are going to work through this. Sex last night wasn't great or sort of a disaster, but it's okay; I love you and I think you are beautiful." Man, it's like you have healed her. Or at least offered healing words.

Scripture says a husband's words can heal his woman. Speak hope and life over her, remind her she is beautiful, loveable, and mostly that she is your dearest friend. If she knows you consider her a dear friend, she knows you won't hurt her, at least not on purpose. You have just calmed her fired-up brain and helped her attach herself to you. You can do this! Trust me, this will make a huge difference in your sexual relationship with your wife. But don't do this to get sex. You are way too mature for that. You love to love her because you love her, not because you want something from her.

One super important thing the woman in the Song of Songs repeatedly advises is, "Oh, let me warn you, sisters in Jerusalem, by the gazelles, yes, by all the wild deer: Don't excite love, don't stir it up, until the time is ripe—and you're ready" (Song of Sol. 3:5). Hmmm—this is what I think she is saying: don't rush intercourse, don't invite him inside of you until you are good and ready and you want him. Don't fake being turned on for his sake. It won't satisfy him. Even those wild deer can tell the difference between a woman who is faking being turned on and a woman who is really turned on and wanting him. Get ripe and ready before you invite him to enter your vagina. You get ripe and ready by plenty of foreplay.

Make it fun. Make it interesting. Get into it. Use lubrication. Don't lie there and expect him to turn you on. You get into it. Help him get you ready to receive him. Be an active lover. Kiss him passionately and deeply. Play with his body, and invite him to play with yours. Ask him to touch you in your favorite ways. Don't hold back. Sex is so good for you. But don't have intercourse if you aren't fully aroused. I can't tell you the women I have had in my office who say, "I never have an orgasm anymore and sex sort of hurts or is uncomfortable."

I ask them, "How long are you giving yourself to get aroused? Are you enjoying ten to twenty minutes of foreplay?"

"Well, no. It's all pretty fast." If that's your answer as well, then you and your husband aren't having mutually pleasurable sex. You are probably servicing him.

Listen, I think a husband and a wife owe each other sex. When you said, "I do," you were promising to be this person's forever sexual partner, to the best of your ability. I get sickness, kids, surgery, and other circumstances that cause sexual pauses. But we can't stay there. Here's the thing: I don't believe in duty sex. Ultimately, duty sex or servicing your man sexually ends up being a pretty empty and eventually a resentment-building experience for both the husband and the wife.

Typically, the belief behind duty sex is, "He needs it and if I don't give it to him at least occasionally he will be tempted and I don't want him cheating." If that is your belief system, that doesn't come from a place of love and redemption, that comes from a place of fear. Deal with the fear so you can truly make love to the man you said, "I do," to. The men I have asked how duty sex feels for them say this, "It's not what I want. It does the job, but I wish she wanted me and I wish I wasn't another chore for her to check off the list." Ouch! Can you hear his hurt?

Men are far more tender than they let us in on. I don't think this is what God wants for any marriage. In 1 Cor. 7:1–7, the Apostle Paul says this:

> Is it a good thing to have sexual relations? Certainly—but only within a certain context. It's good for a man to have a wife, and for a woman to have a husband. Sexual drives are strong, but marriage is strong enough to contain them and provide for a balanced and fulfilling sexual life in a world of sexual disorder. The marriage bed MUST be a place of mutuality—the husband seeking to satisfy his wife, the wife seeking to satisfy her husband. Marriage is a decision to serve the other, whether in bed or out.

Paul makes a great point here, marriage is the willingness to serve another. I think we can serve each other, and sex is the most fulfilling when the husband wants to give his wife pleasure and she wants to give him pleasure. Take pleasure in your spouse's pleasure and you double the pleasure. Paul also affirms that sexual drives are strong. You have complete biblical support to have strong sexual drives. The only caveat is to put those strong sexual urges in the right context: marriage.

Women, don't compare yourself to your husband. Most likely his erections are pretty instant and spontaneous. All he needs is to see you or think about sex and the rocket is ready to launch. Women are different sexually from men. They are just as sexual but need more warm-up time and some inviting to get into their bodies. Men actually become more like females sexually as they age and testosterone levels lower. It can be kind of great because then he needs more play time too. Dr. Rosemary Basson says it something like this, "After having children or after being in a relationship for several years, sex becomes more of a choice for a woman, she slips more into sexual neutrality."[2] What she is saying is that earlier in the relationship you may have had lots of hot passion for your man, then your jets cooled as the years went on.

I noticed when this changed for me. It was between the birth of our second and third son. We had been married for a while, and we were deep into baby land. I thought to myself while vacuuming the family room, *hmmm, where did my* Oh La La *go? I miss that.* What I did notice was that even though I may not have that powerful *Oh La La* of desire, if I engaged with Ron sexually, after a while, I would move from sexually neutral to finding that first gear, then the second, and, *bam*, the third, and we were off to the races. It just took a little longer, but it was still there if I would just remind myself how great it is once I get into it. I think too many women shut down the idea when their husband initiates because she isn't in the mood right then and there.

You may not be, but I want to encourage you to engage and go for it, knowing it will come. Give it time; wait for it. It's always worth it. I frequently ask women, "When you do engage sexually with your man are you glad you did in the end?" Do you ever hear yourself saying, "We should do that more often"? That's because you are sexual and when you are married, the Apostle

Paul, the single guy, says to have sex frequently; it's super good for you.

Married couples who have sex regularly live longer, have better heart health, enjoy a deeper connection, and can let go of annoyances easier. I'm sure someday in heaven, God will give us a million more reasons why He made sex for husband and wife to enjoy and why it was so good for us.

So here is my encouragement to you: Do it. Do it often, as often as is fun. Push yourself a little. Get your groove on. Find your mojo. Don't let this beautiful thing God made die. That's a sad, long, painful death. Fight for it. Don't give up on it. Don't be passive or aggressive about it. Do whatever you have to do to make this work for you both. Talk. Become sexual friends. Turn him on. Turn her on. Get help. Give it your best and your all. Be courageous. Go for it. Seriously, your marriage will be more fun, richer, deeper, sexier, much more connected if you do! It's the only thing you have that is all yours. It's your private heaven on earth. Make out on the couch, in the shower, in the car. Be sexual with each other. Make it all it can be. There are no limits, only the ones you put on it.

A FINAL NOTE

While writing this book my eyes have frequently wandered to a photo of Ron and me with our six grandchildren. We are seated next to each other and he has his arms wrapped around our three grandsons and I have mine wrapped around our three granddaughters. Soon we will welcome another grandchild into our clan. All of our faces are lit up with the shared love we have for one another. Tears fill my eyes as I think about the times we wondered if we would make it, or were tempted to give up. Our love and attachment have held us steady along with the solid arms of the Lord we both love.

Ron and I fell in love in high school and married shortly after we graduated. We were young. We have had to fight for our marriage many times. Just last weekend we hurt each other through a silly misunderstanding. (It didn't seem silly at the time.) But as my eyes wander to this photo reminding me of our history together, I am so grateful we have struggled to create a legacy. You have a legacy to create as well. Just like the characters you have been reading about.

Each of them have choices to make. Will they choose to heal? Will they press in and do the hard work of becoming healthy human beings? Will they have the courage to face the past so it does not define their future? Will they stay lost in sexual confusion or will they make the hard choices needed to heal? It's not easy work and it certainly isn't an automatic given we will truly become adults. Every adult has to work on their character structure, their belief systems, and must work through the history that formed and shaped them.

Ron and I have had our fair share of collected garbage to work through. I grew up in a home with physical, verbal, and sexual abuse, along with emotional neglect. Ron experienced massive amounts of neglect and huge boundary violations. After forty-two years of marriage, we can say, "God is good; trust Him with your past, your present, and your future." Allow Him to search your heart and dig around in the soil of your life. Allow

Him to challenge your character structure and invite him to reveal anything in need of His healing hand.

Every human needs some part of their brain rewired and their heart healed. It's normal. Treat it like it is and dig into becoming the integrated whole human He longs for you to become: free from shame, free from secrets, free from lies. God wants you to live in a wide open space, the space your soul needs to prosper and live—really live.

Acknowledgments

As my husband, Ron, says, "This book has taken a lifetime of *work* to be written." Many have contributed to this journey I have been on. Even though my childhood had its fair share of trauma, I'm grateful for the *grit* I learned from my father and the gentle kindness of my mother.

I am grateful for the influence of the many pastors who have spoken into my life. I would especially like to thank Pastor Book, Pastor Groff, Bill Carmichael, and Brady Boyd.

I have been blessed with wonderful colleagues and professors who have invited me to think, process my issues, and shape my skills as a therapist. I am grateful for the team at the Institute for Sexual Wholeness: Dr. Doug Rosenau, Debra Taylor, Dr. Michael Sytsma, Christopher McCluskey, Dr. Cliff and Joyce Penner, Dr. Mark Yarhouse, and Dr. Wade Hemminger at DBU.

Also, I am thankful for my Townsend Leadership family. I love that we get to do serious life-changing stuff together and laugh until our sides hurt. You are one fun bunch of people! I appreciate the opportunity to work with Dr. Townsend as a Townsend Leadership director in Texas and New York.

To the staff and congregation of Gateway Church, you are a part of this book. Thank you for opportunities to further develop my thinking on the topic of human sexuality. To all of those who attended classes, participated in groups, loved me as I learned, and continued to say how important this topic is—thank you!

Wes Yoder, thank you. You have guided this process with such grace and wisdom. You believed in my writing and your connections and friendship led us to Gary Terashita. Gary, thank you for believing in this project. Thank you for caring about this topic and how it has influenced the world we live in. You and the amazing Regnery team have added to this book and made it all possible. I am forever grateful and humbled to have the support of Regnery Publishing. Sarah Wronko, this book wouldn't exist without you. You have given me endless support and inspiration. You are more than an editor; you are a true friend.

To our precious sons, Aaron, Joshua, Micah, and Jonathan. God does take the lonely and put them into family and you have made for a *wonderful* family! I am blessed to be your mom. You are the best sons a mother could have. You have taught me about love, forgiveness, grace, courage, and joy. I loved watching you grow up to become the men you are. I love the women you picked to make your own families with. Nicole, Lauren, Darcy, and Annie, thank you for being outstanding daughters to Ron and me. You are the ones we didn't give birth to, but we are so happy for the much-needed estrogen and femininity each of you so beautifully bring. To top it all off, you have given us eight grandchildren. Titus, Lola Kate, Gracyn, Sailor, James, Levi, Dottie Lynn, and Scout—well, you are the frosting on the cake!

Lastly, I want to thank the many clients who have given me the opportunity to practice, listen, learn, attune to, hurt with, and watch as they grow and overcome. You inspire me!

Notes

FOUR: LOVE AND LONGING

1. Ted Roberts, found in *Conquer Series: The Battle Plan for Purity* Study Guide by Jeremy and Tiana Wiles (Stuart, FL: KingdomWorks Studios, 2013.

SEVEN: THE GUYS' GROUP

1. Daniel Amen, at the American Association of Christian Counselors conference.

EIGHT: TIME TO HEAL

1. Dallas Willard, *The Great Omission: Reclaiming Jesus's Essential Teachings on Discipleship* (San Francisco: HarperOne, 2006).
2. Eric Barker, "A Neuroscience Researcher Reveals 4 Rituals That Will Make You Happier," *Business Insider*, September

26, 2015, www.businessinsider.com/a-neuroscience-researcher-reveals-4-rituals-that-will-make-a-happier-person-2015-9.

NINE: SEXUAL WHOLENESS SEMINAR

1. "The Porn Phenomenon: The Impact of Pornography in the Digital Age," A Barna Report Produced in partnership with Josh McDowell Ministry, 2016.
2. Ibid.
3. Daniel J. Siegel, *The Mindful Therapist* (New York: W. W. Norton & Company, 2010), 62.
4. See Dozier, Stovall, Albus, and Bates, "Attachment for Infants in Foster Care: The Role of Caregiver State of Mind," 2001.
5. Daniel J. Siegel, "About Interpersonal Neurobiology," http://www.drdansiegel.com/about/interpersonal_neurobiology/.
6. Song by Jimmy Krondes and J. Taylor, 1976.
7. Siegel, *The Mindful Therapist*.

TWELVE: PASSION

1. Paul W. Eastwick and Eli J. Finkel, "The Attachment System in Fledgling Relationships: An Activating Role for Attachment Anxiety," *Journal of Personality and Social Psychology*, 2008, vol. 95: 628–47.
2. Rosemary Basson, "Rethinking Low Sexual Desire in Women," *BJOG: An International Journal of Obstetrics and Gynecology*, vol. 109, issue 4, April 2002: 357–63, onlinelibrary.wiley.com.